Conferring
with Young
Writers

Conferring with Young Writers

What to Do When You Don't Know What to Do

Kristin Ackerman &
Jennifer McDonough

STENHOUSE PUBLISHERS
PORTLAND, MAINE

Stenhouse Publishers
www.stenhouse.com

Library of Congress Cataloging-in-Publication Data

Names: Ackerman, Kristin, 1983- author. | McDonough, Jennifer, 1974- author.
Title: Conferring with young writers : what to do when you don't know what to
    do / Kristin Ackerman and Jennifer McDonough.
Description: Portland, Maine : Stenhouse Publishers, 2016. | Includes
    bibliographical references.
Identifiers: LCCN 2016007223 (print) | LCCN 2016020087 (ebook) | ISBN
    9781625310392 (pbk. : alk. paper) | ISBN 9781625311238 (ebook)
Subjects: LCSH: Composition (Language arts)--Study and teaching (Elementary)
    | English language--Composition and exercises--Study and teaching
    (Elementary) | Individualized instruction. | Teacher-student relationships.
Classification: LCC LB1576 .A384 2016 (print) | LCC LB1576 (ebook) | DDC
    372.62/3--dc23
LC record available at https://lccn.loc.gov/2016007223

Book design by Blue Design (www.bluedes.com)

Manufactured in the United States of America

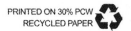
PRINTED ON 30% PCW
RECYCLED PAPER

22 21 20 19 18 17 16   9 8 7 6 5 4 3 2 1

We dedicate this book to all the amazing writers in our lives, especially Banyan, Caroline, Leila, and Will.

CONTENTS

ACKNOWLEDGMENTS

Do you all have any idea how hard it is to write a book when you live in sunny South Florida? There are not many "It's a good day to just stay inside and write" days. We are thrilled with ourselves for actually completing this!

Thank you to Georgia Heard and Karen Basil, who saw the potential in us before we could see it in ourselves. You both taught us to reach for the Brie and never settle for American cheese, and for that we are ever grateful!

Thank you to Bill Varner and the entire Stenhouse team for taking a chance on us and sharing our quest to give teachers a plan for how to feel successful when teaching writing. Thank you, Erin Trainer and the whole copyediting team, for polishing up our writing. We also want to thank Claire Canese Photography for the beautiful pictures.

A huge shout-out to all the student writers who have taught us more than we ever could have taught you; without you this book would not exist.

Thank you to the mentors in our lives: Gail Boushey, Joan Moser, Ellin Keene, Jan Burkins, Kim Yaris, Kathy Collins, Lucy Calkins, Matt Glover, Katie Wood Ray, Brenda Power, Ralph Fletcher, and "the Donalds"—both Graves and Murray. Your work, and the work of so many other educators, inspires us to keep reaching for the next best thing. Thank you, Jess, our friend, running partner, therapist, and coach. We needed every pep talk, every run, and every laugh.

FROM JEN

Well, Kristin, we did it! Without your organized type-A personality, your drive and commitment, and your eternal optimism I'm pretty sure we would still just be talking about this book project instead of writing acknowledgments. I couldn't ask for a better friend or writing partner. Here's to the adventures yet to come!

To the incredible teachers who have surrounded me over the years, cheering me on and challenging me to do better for the kids in my classroom every day—Krista Monahan, Claire Canese, Megan Lilliedahl, Victoria Sloane, Debi Gillert, Lisa Glogower, Megan Moffit, Laura Chesnes, Tara Hughes, Sandy Held, Casey Engelhardt, Audra Cato, Kara Koetter, Stacey Hill, and the rest of The Benjamin School family—thank you. Also, a big thank-you to two amazing administrators—Robyn Quaid and Kristen Sheehan—who understand that I need to "push the boundaries" every once in a while in order to spread my wings and grow. Learning from mistakes makes me a better teacher.

A thank-you goes out to Ray and Tarry Graziotto, who gave me a place to write. Without your cozy guesthouse, I would still be on Chapter 1. The snacks helped, too!

Thank you to my amazing Michigan family, who surrounds me and tries to understand the craziness of my life without judging. Mom and Dad, you are always there to pick up the balls as they are dropping and help me get back to some sort of sanity. Kate and Abby, you have always supported me and been such great cheerleaders for all the crazy things I take on. I am blessed to have such a family, and that includes all of you! To all the McDonoughs as well, thanks for always being there when I am having my proud moments. What would I do without my Florida family?

And finally, to Brian, Will, and Caroline: Will and Caroline, thank you for your patience, understanding, and support as Mommy worked hard to write this book. My hope is that my hard work will show you how to go for everything you want in life as well. Have big dreams, then go bigger! Brian, you took on a lot of weekends as a single dad. Thanks for signing up for this crazy ride and understanding that I just can't say no to big opportunities. I love you. Okay, family, the book is finally done (until the next one), and no, Will, we didn't write five books, just one, even though I know it felt like that sometimes!

FROM KRISTIN

We all need a "Better Than Me," a person we spend as much time with as possible because we know they are so much better than we are. Jen, you are my "Better Than Me"; you constantly challenge me to grow, to dig deeper, to ask big questions, to reflect, and to implement change. It is such an honor to know you and call you my friend. We have worked so hard together, even though our husbands joked that our meetings were an excuse to drink a glass of wine or go to the spa. We should really go to the spa now that we have finished the book!

I want to thank the many amazing teachers, mentors, and administrators I have worked with. To Robyn Quaid, Karen Basil, Kristen Sheehan, Krista Monahan, Lindsay Davidson, Susan Keller, Susan Bickel, Peg Meehan, Carole Ann Vaughan, Tara Hughes, Teresa Dabrowski, Lisa Arline, Jamie Boykin, Alyssa Feck, Diona Kurz, Lisa Glogower, Debi Gillert, Chelsea Rogers, and Kelly Murray: thank you for letting me hash out ideas and try new things, and for helping me to grow and learn.

To my very big and very supportive family, thank you for being such an incredible village. I couldn't have done it without your help! You have all cared for the kids so that I could pursue my professional goals and forgiven me when I haven't managed to call you back or have been late with a birthday gift. Mom and Lori, you both set the bar really high; this book is my humble attempt to try to keep up with all your accomplishments. Dad, I wish that I could have put this into your hands. You and Mom worked so hard to help me learn how to read, and you thought I would never be a reader; it turns out that I am not only a reader but also a writer. Papa, you have always cheered me on and celebrated my accomplishments. Thank you for being a great stepdad and the best grandpa to my kids.

To the three most important people in my life, Justin, Banyan, and Leila: Justin, I have always teased you that the best things in life come from Texas and that you are lucky to have me, but the truth is that having you for a best friend is the greatest gift I have ever been given. Thank you for all the weekends you let me disappear so that Jen and I could write, and thank you for always supporting me and having such a great attitude about it. Banyan and Leila, you have taught me so much about what really matters. You have inspired me to want to be the very best mom, teacher, and writer I can be. You are both so full of life and joy and adventure. I can't wait to see what stories you will write and share as you continue to grow.

INTRODUCTION

You know the deep, reflective thinking we try to have with our colleagues during five minutes of kid-free time as we walk back from the copy machine and see another adult for the first time that day? That is where our journey started. We happened to see each other on a day when writing workshop was not going well in either of our classrooms. The conversation began.

Jen: Ugh . . . Writing time was a mess in first grade today!

Kristin: (*nodding*) I know. It isn't any easier in third grade!

In unison: What the heck are we going to do??

We knew we couldn't continue the way things were going and knew we needed to spend our time more wisely.

What *were* we going to do? We needed a plan. We decided to meet once every few weeks during our planning time, after school, or whenever we passed each other in the hall to start brainstorming what was going well and what we needed to work on. We also talked a lot on the phone after our kids were in bed that first year, trying to hash out ideas. We started by writing down our questions and concerns around writing in our classrooms. Here are some of them:

- What is essential to teaching kids about writing?
- Are there specific foundational strategies I should be teaching? What are they?

- When I teach genre units of study, why can't kids transfer what they learn and know about writing from one unit to another?
- We know anchor charts are a valuable resource for helping kids retain and grow thinking as we progress through a writing unit, but why can't the students retain the writing strategies they learn in a unit once the chart comes down? In conferences, my suggestions seem more to do with whatever genre kids are writing about that day. Should I instead have clear, comprehensive goals that apply to all genres?
- If I don't feel like I am a good writer myself, how can I be sure about what I should teach the writers in my classroom?
- What should conversations with my kids about their writing sound like?

As we talked over the course of that year, we realized that maybe we weren't the only teachers with a lot of unanswered questions. When the two of us were in school, the message was that either you are a good writer or you are not, and we both felt like we fell into the "not" category. Sure, we had written our share of five-paragraph essays, book reviews, and outlines, but we had never felt like we were *writers*. We hadn't learned much about the qualities of good writing, such as elaboration, voice, and structure. Our teachers hadn't taught us how to look at a great piece of writing and break it down into the qualities and craft that could show us why we loved the writing. We hadn't been taught to ask questions like these:

> "What kind of lead did the author use to get me so engaged right from the beginning?"

> "What strategies of elaboration does this writer use to make me feel like I am right in the story?"

> "How do writers come up with ideas for things to write about?"

The qualities of writing are many and can vary (Routman 2005; Culham 2005; Graves and Kittle 2005; Calkins 2013), but we have found that what matters most for us in crafting writing are structure, conventions, focus, voice, and elaboration. These qualities of good writing are used in any genre of writing and provide clear goals for instruction.

Our college teaching courses taught us about the pedagogy of teaching, reading theory, and how to teach children to read, but not much was included about how to teach young children to be writers. It was not until people like Georgia Heard and Lucy Calkins entered our lives to say, "You can be a writer and here is how" that we realized good writing is simply a matter of exposure and learning how writers go about crafting writing. Anyone can be a good writer with the proper training.

When we looked at the work going on in our classrooms and the questions we had, we also realized that many of our concerns were focused on what to teach writers to help them grow. This got us thinking that the biggest and most powerful change we could make could be in our *conferring time* with writers. This is the time when we get kids alone or in strategy groups and delve into their writing. We take the words of Lucy Calkins to heart when she says,

> To an outside observer, I suspect that conferring with young writers looks like No Big Deal. But in the classrooms of some teachers, children grow in leaps and bounds, while in the classrooms of other teachers, children make only modest gains. I am utterly convinced that the difference has everything to do with the teacher's abilities to confer. If a teacher can listen to a writer talk about her writing, and then can skim what the child has done so far and intervene in ways that lift the level of not only the piece of writing but of the child's work on future pieces, that teacher's conferences are a Very Big Deal. That teacher's children will learn to write in powerful ways. (Calkins, Hartman, and White 2005, 3–4)

Conferring is a time to differentiate our instruction to meet a child's particular needs. Instead of relying on the child to actually listen during a whole-group lesson and understand it, we can say to that child, "Here is what is working for you. Let me show you something that will make it even better." There is less room for confusion or error while conferring; there are no worries that the child might think we are teaching to the friend sitting next to him on the rug. The child gets that the work to be done, the lesson to be learned, is his and his alone. This is where specific and powerful teaching and learning occur. So we decided that if we could change the way we confer with young writers, we could answer a lot of our questions and help our writers grow.

As we taught our students and continued to talk with each other between classes, these questions and concerns swirled and grew in our minds. So, we decided to begin a journey. A journey toward answering our questions and quelling our concerns. A journey to figure out what the heck to do. A journey to take the writing process and qualities of good writing and make them transparent so that every teacher, both novice and expert, can feel successful when teaching writing, especially when it comes to conferring. Our goal was to make these strategies transparent and attainable for our students as well, so that young writers would be able to articulate the writing strategies that helped them grow and become better writers. We intentionally use the term *strategies* because it means "a plan, method, or series of maneuvers or stratagems for obtaining a specific goal or result," which is what we are trying to do. To put a focus on the writing skills that really matter. To ensure that our conferring is less random and more thoughtful and purposeful as we help young writers move forward. We want our teaching to be less caught up in genre and show teachers and kids how most writing strategies can be used, just like most reading strategies can be, no matter what genre you are writing or reading. We want to take away the belief that you are either good at writing or you are not. We want to help teachers develop "writers" in their classrooms and not just "kids who can write." There is a difference.

As you read, you will also see three core beliefs about writing embedded in everything we do:

1. All children can learn.

2. Children develop differently.

3. We have a responsibility as educators to constantly grow, both professionally and personally.

These core beliefs ultimately drive every decision we make when it comes to writing in our classrooms. The ideas we share in this book will all wrap themselves around those beliefs.

This book began with trying to answer the question, "How can we spend our writing time more effectively with kids?" We believe it is through powerful conferring. This book is a culmination of our work and thinking on how to confer effectively and powerfully with young children about their writing.

WE DIDN'T SAY THIS WOULD BE EASY

One day Kristin walked into a colleague's room and found her excited to share a "cute" writing chart she had found on Pinterest. Kristin, sensing her excitement, went right over to read the chart and exclaimed, "Oh, you're trying out Ruth Culham's work around six traits. Great stuff."

"Wait, who is Ruth Culham?" the teacher questioned. "This is from Pinterest from [so-and-so's] board!" What the teacher did not realize was that "so-and-so" had taken Ruth's work and moved the words around in a different order. Because Kristin's colleague had not read Ruth's books, she did not realize that there was actual research, the part that really matters, behind the chart. As a good friend always reminded us, "Those who do the most work, do the most learning." Kristin's colleague, unfortunately, hadn't done the work. This story illustrates a trend we see education gravitating toward. In a Pinterest and Teachers Pay Teachers world we don't want to lose sight of what each of us, as educators, brings to the table. Nor do we want to forget the importance of understanding the research behind the instructional decisions we make every day. Don't get us wrong, we love all the online tools that are right at our fingertips. But a cute worksheet with special font is never going to replace the need for a teacher to coach his or her students with research-based instruction that works. We agree with Ann Marie Corgill when she says in her wonderful book *Of Primary Importance*, "I believe so much of what's happening in education today, so much of what's being published, is giving teachers permission not to think anymore. It is my hope and my sincere request that you think of this book as a friend standing by to cheer you on in your classroom. Use it as a resource . . . Be your own teacher of children" (2008, 3).

We are starting to notice this more and more in our society, where information is a click away and the new teaching mentality is, "Why work so hard on it myself when I know someone out there already did it?" We get the sense of being overwhelmed that comes with teaching; we know there is never enough time to do all we want to do. We both work full-time and have young children. No one wants a quick fix more than we do some days. Our concern is that research-based instruction is being replaced by "quick-click" instruction and is enabling teachers to teach without knowing the what or why behind what they are doing. Teachers need a plan, a direction, and a better way to successfully teach children than blindly copying something that leads to a lack of understanding for the teacher and the students.

So, to the tech-savvy teachers of the world we say, "Way to go." We are striving to use as many online tools as we can, too, but the cute fonts and worksheets are a tool, *not* a curriculum. Technology and chevron borders cannot drive instruction; quick clicks should not become a curriculum. Teachers need to be creators of the work they do every day with students, and doing it with grit is how they become their very best. No one can become a better tennis player by watching videos on YouTube. You have to get out and play. You have to experience the challenges and mistakes that come with the game. Each game will be different based on the opponent and what they bring. We would argue the same is true for teaching and, specifically, conferring during writing. You have to be in it, really in it, every day, trying to learn from the mistakes and challenges that come with conferring to truly be on your game. There is no Pinterest board or Teacher Pay Teachers account that can take the place of that experience.

As we have struggled through our journey, we have learned a lot through our mistakes and challenges. When we were new teachers we often felt like we were showing our commitment by how late we stayed at school every night or how cute our classrooms looked. As we grew professionally and our thinking shifted, we realized that the important work we do at school happens when we are face-to-face with kids. The organizing and planning outside the classroom allows us to be focused and productive, but the heart of what we do can happen only with kids in the room. We have learned that what we say (or what we are smart enough not to say) in a five-minute conference or during a quick strategy group can have a huge impact on our writers.

We have taught writing with grit over the past few years. We have taken the time and energy to figure out how to do it better than we did the day before. We won't be luring you or your students in with cute fonts but we will share everything that has worked for us. If you have ever avoided teaching writing because you were afraid that you didn't know what you were doing, this book is for you. If you have ever looked at a child's writing and felt totally and utterly lost, this book is for you. If you feel comfortable conferring only when you talk about capitals and periods, this book is for you. We don't pretend to have it all figured out, but we do know that writers are not born; writing is a learned skill. We believe that it is possible to sit down with writers and confer successfully when we are aware of the bigger goals we want our writers to achieve. We hope that this book will make you feel the same.

We are hoping that by the end of this journey we will have formed a community of educators not only invested in teaching children how to think and work through writing projects, but also writing ourselves, for this is the only way we will *truly* know how to teach writers. In *The Book Whisperer*, Donalyn Miller tells us, "The reality is that you cannot inspire others to do what you are not inspired to do yourself" (2009, 118). So we say to you, just as it was said to us, "Of course you are a writer and teacher of writing—here's how!"

Now, let's begin!

CHAPTER 1

THE ELEMENTS OF CONFERRING WELL: BUILDING TRUST

We would be remiss if we did not first focus on what we feel is the most important aspect of conferring: developing a trusting relationship. The relationships we build and share with our young writers become the foundation of our writing work together. Before we can even begin to delve into writing conversations, we need to build trust. We are asking kids to put themselves out there when they write about their feelings, their knowledge of letters and letter sounds, their knowledge of writing, and their beliefs about the world. It is no wonder that many adults, including teachers, do not want to write themselves. It is hard to put yourself out there. So we have to be careful. If we do not build positive relationships with children first, they will shut down as writers. It's just too personal. When we thought together about the ways in which we build positive relationships with our kids, we noticed a few overarching beliefs that help strengthen relationships and fuel successful writing conversations:

Writing teachers need to write.

We build from strengths.

We create compliments that are lasting.

We listen, *really* listen, to what a child is saying.

We notice and connect with our writers.

WRITING TEACHERS NEED TO WRITE

Jen was recently at a conference where she asked the teachers in the room how many of them write themselves. Out of fifty-eight teachers, two raised their hands. We see this as one of the biggest problems teachers create for themselves when it comes time to confer. In order to confer well, there needs to be an empathy for how it feels to be a writer. A teacher who writes—and we aren't saying you have to be a good writer—is able to talk a student through strategies and help him or her through trouble spots because they both walk in the same writing shoes. We all know experience brings wisdom, and we advocate for you to write yourself so you can truly coach your writers in explicit ways. We are not proposing you start writing a novel in your free time between 1:00 and 3:00 a.m. You can begin simply by attempting the kind of writing you are going to ask the kids to do before you start a unit and notice what goes well for you and where your struggles are. Maybe you start a journal or a blog. Even thinking about the emails you send and how you craft and revise them with your audience in mind can be enough. Now that we both are writing more frequently in our personal lives, we are able to have honest conversations with the kids in our classrooms about what it feels like to lose focus in a piece or about the confusion caused through too much elaboration. We know what it feels like to revise our writing work over and over again. We share our writing struggles and successes with the kids so that we are a part of the writing community and not just on the outside looking in. We have gone from saying things like, "Because I said so" to more empathetic statements such as, "I know that it can be overwhelming to figure out how to make your piece better, but let me show you one easy thing you might try here that worked for me." Don't just be a teacher of writing; be a writer yourself in any way that you can. Your ability to talk kids through their writing will improve and your relationship with the kids will deepen because they know you are in it with them.

Build from Strengths

When Georgia Heard and Jen decided to write *A Place for Wonder: Reading and Writing Nonfiction in the Primary Grades* (2009), Jen was happily clueless as a writer. She had never written anything besides a college paper and was oblivious to the enormity of the task to which she had eagerly agreed. All Jen knew was that the work they were doing in her classroom was magical and she wanted to share it. The first draft of writing she gave to Georgia was single-spaced, in a cutesy font, and there were no paragraphs. She had absolutely no idea what she was doing. Somewhere in all of that, Georgia found the good parts. She was able to look past the convention work that needed some *serious* help and see what it was Jen was trying to convey. Whenever she read Jen's writing, she always reminded her how far she had come, noticed the ways in which Jen was growing in her ability to share her thinking, and had a kind suggestion for how she could improve for next time. Jen should have been scared to death to be coauthoring a book with such an accomplished writer, yet she was never made to feel like she wasn't good enough to be writing alongside Georgia. One of the biggest reasons Jen was able to accomplish what she did was the relationship. When Georgia gave her suggestions for ways to improve, Jen was thrilled for the feedback and never felt intimidated or defeated. Georgia and Jen had a positive relationship from the beginning of their friendship. She always knew that Georgia was there to help her grow and learn and had her best interests at heart. Isn't this how we want all our students to feel?

Knowing what worked for Jen and Georgia, we found that one of the most important ways to build relationships with our young writers was to intentionally look past the convention errors such as capitalization and punctuation and see who they really were as writers. We tried to see the good in every writer—what they brought to the blank page—and to find ways we could offer guidance going forward in their writing. As teachers, we often see only the developmental spelling errors, lack of punctuation, and pages of repeated words and exclamation marks. You know what we mean: "It was fun soooo-oooooo-ooooo-oooooo-ooooo-oooooo-ooooo much fun. Really fun" (see Figure 1.1). We believe that because punctuation is the easiest thing to notice and fix, teachers tend to fixate on it. We can quickly point out missing periods and watch a child add them in right before our eyes. Voila! We get to walk away feeling like we made a difference because the child actually did what we asked him or her to do. But is that always the best use of our expertise and the best way to help a writer grow? We think not.

Katherine Bomer supports us when she says, "I wanted to hold up the sparest, most inelegant, illegible pieces of student writing and say, "Look at this! Look at the fresh, original way this young person spoke of loss; the way this piece about bodily functions made a group of teachers laugh and laugh. I wanted to teach how to see jewels in all students' writing, no matter what difficulties with language use they might exhibit" (2010, 162). Teaching a child to revise for greater depth in writing is what will ultimately make the biggest difference. The surface-level writing skills can be edited in final draft.

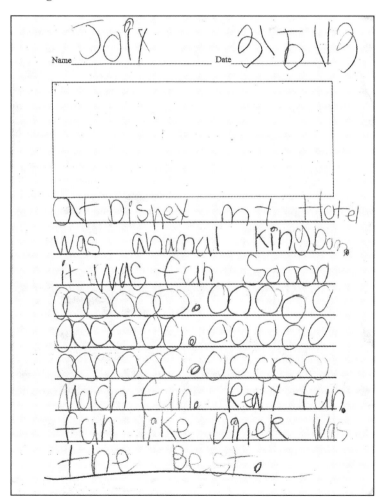

FIGURE 1.1
Joix's Writing Piece

It is easy to look at student writing and notice what is going wrong; the challenge is to identify what is going well and teach to a writer's strengths. We try to stop ourselves from looking at the child and saying, "Argh, are you kidding me?" and instead say, "Looks like you were *really* happy at Disney; the drawing out of the word *so* definitely shows that!" Then we talk with that child about other ways writers can show happiness in their writing pieces and hope that in the next piece she uses two *so*'s instead of seventeen because she now knows as a writer she can include details that show the happiness instead of just using the same word over and over. This is how we build the relationship first. By seeing the good, the best try, and moving forward from there, kids begin to trust that we see what they are trying to do. Without the relationship first, writing can become a time of stress for kids. A time of always feeling like something is missing instead of celebrating what is already there. In his book *Write Like This: Teaching Real-World Writing Through Modeling and Mentor Texts*, Kelly Gallagher says, "Unfortunately, I think a lot of teachers spend much of their time interacting with students' writing by pointing out what is wrong with it." He adds, "The focus should always be on what good writers do, not on the mistakes writers make" (2011, 235). How defeating would it have been for Jen if Georgia focused only on what her writing was lacking? When kids aren't writing during writing time, we need to reflect and ask ourselves questions like, *What does my conferring sound like with this child?* and *Am I encouraging and nudging in a positive way or focusing only on what is missing and the mistakes being made?*

Katherine Bomer tells us, "My hope is that as teachers we respond to all students' writing with astonished, appreciative, awestruck eyes. But we can't create this kind of writing response if we don't first 'fall in love' with our students' quirky, unconventional, and culture-infused texts" (2010, 7). This is what we need to do for kids before we get into the nitty-gritty and work of teaching craft in writing. We need to notice the strengths, another essential to building a trusting relationship.

CREATE LASTING COMPLIMENTS

A key part of building from strengths is to come up with lasting compliments. In *Writing Workshop: The Essential Guide*, Ralph Fletcher and JoAnn Portalupi tell us, "Most young writers work behind a window of vulnerability that is tightly shut and locked. When you give them specific praise, they open that window a tiny crack" (2001, 51). Once you have identified an area of writing where the child has done well, the second step is to craft a compliment that celebrates the strength so that you up the chances that the child will use what you notice is going well again and again. When writers are putting so much of themselves out there on paper, we need to appreciate the risk taking and celebrate it, not shut them down. Take the time to point out what is going well before you move on to next steps for growth. When a strategy is disguised within a celebration, the child doesn't even know they are being taught. We know with our own children at home that when something is our idea the kids want nothing to do with it. When we trick them into thinking something is their idea, they are all over it! Reverse psychology, the best parent trick we know. Complimenting can be just like that. When you skip the compliment the tendency is to jump right to what they need next and not celebrate what is going right. In *One to One: The Art of Conferring with Young Writers,* Lucy Calkins and her colleagues remind us how important it is to compliment writers in an explicit, teachable way. "The challenge for us as teachers is to notice a very specific way in which the child has succeeded, and then to phrase a compliment in such a way that the child knows it is something she should carry into her writing work in general" (Calkins, Hartman, and White 2005, 9). They talk about how a compliment is essentially another teaching point to help children see that their writing attempts are thoughtful and worthwhile. Following are some examples of compliments:

- So smart the way you used the word wall to spell words correctly so anyone can read your great writing!
- When you use different kinds of punctuation like ellipses it really makes your reader want to read more.
- When you tell the reader what you were thinking as you were on the roller coaster it helps the reader be in the moment with you.
- I am noticing that you are talking to your reader. I found myself laughing out loud; what a great way to connect with your reader! Writers do that all the time.

Compliments are yet another important way to build trusting relationships and have meaningful conversations with our students.

LISTEN TO WHAT A CHILD IS SAYING

In 2012, we were lucky enough to present our ideas about conferring with young writers with Georgia Heard at the National Council of Teachers of English (NCTE) convention. Georgia reminded all of us that another essential of conferring is listening. She talked about conferences with young writers being like a "listening tour," where you go from child to child really listening to what they are saying to you. When a teacher truly listens to a child read and talk about writing, the best teaching can begin. Fletcher and Portalupi (2001), too, remind us that conferring starts with deep listening. We have to shake off our own school experiences of "the classic school paradigm in which teachers talk and students listen" (49). Many times the rush of time and pressure to meet with kids can put teachers into a checklist mode instead of a responding mode. Our heads are filled with lists like the following:

- Capitals at the beginning? Check!
- Punctuation? Check!
- They have actually written something? Check!
- Does it make sense? Check!

Then we dive in with a plan to "fix" this child's writing. This may leave kids feeling like they are a product of an assembly line, pushed through the system and then spit out at the end with a perfect writing product that looks just like the writing products of the kids sitting on either side of them. Lucy Calkins asks,

> Why is it so difficult to give a simple human response [to a child's writing]? I think it is because we try so hard to be helpful we forget to be real. Especially when we first learn to confer we often worry so much about asking the right questions that we forget to listen. We focus on asking the questions that will draw out information, not realizing that it is the listening that creates a magnetic force between writer and audience. The force of listening will draw words out. (1994, 232)

This could be where the real writing begins. So what if the conversation focuses on listening to the writer instead? Lucy Calkins and her colleagues from the Reading and Writing Project taught us to begin with asking, "What are you working on as a writer today?" and then to shut our mouths and open our ears. Another way to get a child talking is to use open-ended questions like the following:

"What feels good about your writing today?"

"What are you trying that's new in your writing?"

"Are there any places in your writing you want to work on?"

The goal of any question you ask is to get the writer talking. When you hold back and listen, you can get a sense of what this child knows as a writer—what he or she can articulate but maybe doesn't know how to execute yet. You can respond with a nudge instead of a push. As Jen wrote in an article about reading, "It is more important than ever that we take time to stop and figure out what our kids *really* know and not what the standards, curriculum, and testing tell us they *should* know" (2012, 31). When you truly listen, you can find out what the child actually knows and start from there.

Another way to train yourself to listen is to close your eyes when you confer with a child. When it comes to teaching we have really seen only a few teachers who have that magical ability to shut everything out and focus on one child at a time. The reality is that the majority of us are snapping our fingers at one kid, giving the stink eye to another, and frustrated that Stevie is out of his seat again, all while trying to confer with the child sitting next to us. Filtering to an elementary school teacher can sometimes feel like an impossible concept!

One day, in a moment of pure exhaustion and inability to deal with everything swirling around her, Jen just closed her eyes and listened to a child read his writing. The most amazing thing happened. By closing her eyes she was able to block out the visual noise around her and focus on the actual words, the bigger things and important things like elaboration, focus, and voice. Her eyes were closed. She could not see the convention issues that most of the time she would obsess over. She was able to focus on things that *really* mattered in the child's piece. For example, Jen was able to show the writer places where he had slowed down the writing using descriptive words that helped her picture how he felt going down a waterslide. Instead of focusing on missed capitals at the beginning of sentences, she was also able to point out another place in his writing where he might use the same strategy. When you listen to children read their work with your eyes closed, you hear the tone and rhythm of the work. You hear what they are trying do as writers to convey their thoughts and don't worry so much at first about how it "looks" on the paper. (We can always edit later!) This is an easy way to celebrate what is going well and ignore the trap of noticing what is not.

NOTICE AND CONNECT WITH WRITERS

As much as we wish that we could meet with every writer every day, we know that it is unrealistic. However, we can communicate and build relationships with our writers even if we do not confer with them right then and there. As we are walking toward our next conference we can make eye contact and smile at a student to encourage her to keep going. We can touch a shoulder or the top of a writer's head to send a message that says, "Hey, I notice you!" We can tap on a writing piece and smile at the writer who is chatting away with a friend to remind him or her to get back on track or give a thumbs-up sign to Bryce across the room because you see her getting right to work. These are effective ways to manage our students and, more important, to remind them that we notice them and we care enough to notice. These little nonverbal cues keep the relationship with the writer going even if we are not meeting with him or her that day.

We also build relationships with our writers by getting to know them as people. We want to know what they do after school, who their friends are, what their family dynamics are, and even what they dislike or fear. We get to know our students during morning meetings, on the playground, and at lunch. Brief conversations don't take a lot of effort, but over time they can teach us a lot about our students. Kristin talked to Johnny about his fishing trips with his dad at lunch and observed Lexi's fierce competitive nature and her athletic ability on the playground. Jen knows that Lizzie and Mia will always want to write about their friend Katie, whom they have missed terribly since she moved away, and that Kai can write about the ocean and sea life in ways no one else in the class can. Building relationships takes time but observation and conversation can teach us a lot if we are paying attention. In our experience it takes at least a few months of noticing, of greeting kids at the door to talk about what happened the day before, of remembering and celebrating the occasions of their lives, or of showing your delight over the things that come to school in their pockets before you begin to see them let go in writing conferences. A little bit at a time.

FIND THE JOY

Finally, after reading the work of Ayres and Overman on how to celebrate writers, we would be remiss if we did not add one more way we build a relationship with our writers—joy.

They end their book with the idea that teachers who want their students to grow as writers and feel good about the work that is being done need to choose joy because, "This is the heart of celebration. We choose joy about the excess of periods in a student's writing, because a month ago there were none. We choose joy about the three meager lines of writing, because yesterday there were crushed pencil points and tears. We choose joy about the misspellings, because all the sight words are accurate. In the face of so much need, we can make a choice to celebrate" (Ayres and Overman 2013, 87–88). If we decide to be joyful about the writing that is being done in the classroom, how can writers not want to write and grow as writers? How can they not trust a teacher who is their cheerleader first and coach second?

Building trust with our writers happens inside and outside writing workshop and it is something that we continue to work at all year. We have to be able to identify what our writers are doing well, compliment them, and keep the relationship going by getting to know them as people. Relationships, trust, and joy are the first steps to helping writers grow. Without these as a foundation, the writers in our classrooms would not trust, would not try, and would not grow.

CHAPTER 2

OVERVIEW: THE THREE Fs

As we were thinking through how to improve our conferring with young writers, we flew together to Florida from the National Council of Teachers of English conference (NCTE) in Las Vegas with nothing but strapped-in sit-down time. We each brainstormed what we thought was essential to our conferring work and shared it to see if we could find some common threads. We noticed as we compared notes that what we had in common were what we now call the three Fs—frequency, focus, and follow-up. What became very clear to us is that the ways we set up our classrooms—the structure, management style, skills taught, and modes of assessment—are determined by these three big threads. By keeping these three overarching goals in mind, we can think through what we are trying to accomplish every day in a logical, structured way. The three Fs now frame the way we approach writing in our classrooms.

INCREASING FREQUENCY

Frequency was the first aspect we noticed as we shared our notes with each other. The only way we could meet with writers with any amount of frequency was to have a strong structure set up to manage the classroom. We know that kids in kindergarten through second grade are going to have less stamina to write. It is key to use management techniques that extend writing time so we can meet with more kids each day. In grades three through five, most students can write for longer periods of time, but we need to make sure that we use the time wisely. Even if we weren't able to revisit the same strategy or goal we had discussed in a previous conference, the frequency with which we met with a child was instrumental in building a positive relationship because we earned the child's trust. Meeting with a child frequently is a way to say, I notice you as a writer and you matter. In order to build in time to meet with kids one-on-one it is essential to build up the independence and stamina of all the writers in the room. No matter what curriculum you use to teach the kids during your writing time, they have to be independently writing for the teacher to be able to meet with kids in any capacity about their writing. To facilitate productive, independent writing time while we are conferring with individual kids, we establish a predictable routine, have materials organized and accessible, and provide lots of choice.

FOCUS

The next goal we realized that we were both striving for was making sure our conferences had a *focus*. We wanted to help young writers figure out what was going well for them, and then focus on work that could help them grow as writers. Once we helped our writers set a goal, we could focus on that goal with them. Until we started thinking about focus, our writing conferences tended to be scattered. We frequently tried to teach too many things at once, bounced from one thing to the next, focused too much on conventions, or ended up doing all the work for the student. This totally confused our young writers and left them with no place to start.

Recently, Jen was at her seven-year-old's baseball practice. She overheard one of the coaches talking to a player on the team. He was saying things like, "Make sure you plant that back foot," "Choke up on the bat more," "Straighten out your feet," and "Hip back and swing through."

The player's mom, overhearing all of this in the bleachers, went down to the fence when the coach walked away and said quietly to her son, "Just take a deep breath and do what feels good to you for now."

She could sense how overwhelming all those directions were for him and we're sure she was worried that in trying to attempt all those strategies, he would lose what was already going well with his batting. Jen watched the player take a deep breath and walk to home plate looking a little less defeated than he had the moment before. The same could be said for some of our writing conferences. There were times (and still are; we are *so* not perfect at this) when we sound just like the well-meaning coach. "Don't forget your punctuation. Oops, now you need a capital here to start the sentence. Don't forget that you need an *e* on the end to make that first vowel say its name. You know how to spell *they*!" Pointing out too many things at once leaves kids overwhelmed and they take nothing away from the conferences but the feeling that they just aren't good writers. Our challenge is to select one thing to teach in a conference. We then model that quality of good writing, show the writer mentor texts that make use of the quality, help the writer see places in his writing where the quality would work, and then walk away to give him time to figure out how to use the strategy in his own writing. Then the next time we see him, we talk about the strategy again and again until we see he has command of it. Then we move on to something else. By focusing on one strategy for a longer amount of time, we give the writer time to play with it and figure out how it works before we start giving him five other things to think about. Lucy Calkins, in *The Art of Teaching Writing,* reminds us that we want to teach the writer, not the writing (1994). This is an essential concept to keep in the forefront of your mind as you confer. When we focus on the specific piece of writing the writer is doing that day and not on a global quality of good writing, it is difficult for him to see how these concepts transfer to a new writing piece. The child gets the sense that what is being taught matters only in what he is currently working on. When we started thinking about focus, it was easier for us to get in and out of a conference by keeping it centered on a quality of good writing that the writer could use no matter what genre he was working on. The qualities of good writing we chose became a great way for us to focus our conferences.

FOLLOW-UP

Follow-up was the third goal we identified. It was important to both of us that when we modeled a strategy for a child, we followed up to see how the strategy was working; that is, we looked for evidence in the writing that the strategy was being used. This is where assessment and accountability come into play. It is human nature to prioritize, and we learn very quickly to avoid or ignore directions when we know that the person of authority will not follow up with us. We all need accountability no matter what the task.

During Kristin's first year of teaching she broke her nose surfing. After waiting two weeks to let the swelling go down, she went in for surgery. After the surgery the doctor placed a small cast on her nose and told her to take the cast off in two weeks. Being the exercise-aholic that she is, her first question was, "When can I run again?" The doctor looked at her like she was crazy. "You can't run for *at least* six weeks," he replied. To Kristin, this was an eternity. After just a few days, knowing she shouldn't, she drove home from school and put on her running shoes and headed out for a few miles. She justified it by telling herself she wouldn't go very far or very fast. Nobody had to know what she was doing. Well, her husband came home early, and as he was pulling into the neighborhood, he caught her. He took one look at her and kept driving. His face said it all and she so knew she was busted. The reality is, though, she felt like she could do what she wanted to because nobody was going to follow up. Her doctor had no way of knowing if she ran or not, so not listening to his directions felt like an option. Isn't that what we all do when there isn't accountability? We eat that yummy chocolate cake instead of an apple when no one's watching. We spend our money on the cute dress instead of saving for future possible car repair bills. We go for a run after surgery, even though it may not be what is best for our body.

The same is true in the classroom. When we first started teaching writing we quickly realized that we had a problem. As we were conferring, our students nodded their heads, said what they thought we wanted to hear, and then they went back to doing whatever they wanted. Our writers were not improving even when we did manage to teach them something really important. Even the most diligent, hardworking, self-motivated kids were not trying out what we were teaching consistently because they knew that our follow-up was more than a bit sporadic. At the time we were still trying to figure out how to document what we had taught each child and how to then use that documentation to follow up.

When we started following up with our students, the culture of our classrooms changed. The kids seemed to take writing more seriously, and authentic conversations became the norm during writing workshop. Accountability comes with follow-up.

When Kristin met with Johnny, one of her very reluctant writers, and asked him to show her the leads he had tried out the day before, he looked at her with a sheepish grin and said, "Oh, you really meant that you wanted me to try out three?" She responded yes and told him she was giving him a ten-minute deadline. Ten minutes later she sat down with him again and he had three leads. It took only a few conferences like this for Johnny to figure out that it was more work and more pressure to avoid Kristin than to just try out what she was teaching him. Kids need to know that we will follow up with them and that they will be held accountable.

The big ideas of frequency, focus, and follow-up provide the framework for everything we do with young writers in our classrooms and provide the framework for this book. We elaborate on each in the succeeding chapters as we turn to the nitty-gritty: the what, the how, and the why of guiding young writers. When working with young writers, here's what you can do when you don't know what to do!

CHAPTER 3

Frequency: Maximizing the Time We Work with Students

When you begin to consider the many specific goals and strategies we offer to teach to the writers in your classroom, you may think, "Great, I will have all this good stuff I can use, but how am I supposed to do this when other kids are constantly interrupting me as I confer??" You are not alone.

The first F stands for the idea of frequency, or finding ways to meet with your kids more often. The hardest part of what we do as classroom teachers is find the time to teach all we want to teach and meet with kids as often as we would like. It seems like there is never enough time. We have learned over the years of teaching writing skills to young children that the more often we can meet with a child and address the specific needs of the child, as opposed to the whole-group "spray and pray," the bigger the impact we can have. The challenging part is always figuring out how to find the time. We all know the joke about having school run until seven o'clock at night to fit it all in. But what we really know, when we sit and reflect on our teaching, is that we need to be more intentional about *how* the time in our classroom is used.

When we sat down to brainstorm ways to meet with kids more often, we realized that most of what we do comes down to management. The way we structure our writing time, the procedures we put in place, the routines we set up at the beginning of the year, and the ways we check in that keep these routines in place all lead to independence. Once you can get the kids to become independent, you find yourself with the time you need to meet with individuals and smaller groups of students more often. This all begins during the launch of your writing time in the beginning of the year. What you model and expect at the beginning of the year will impact the frequency with which you will be able to meet with students for the rest of the year. Answering big questions such as *How will students manage materials? What will they do if they encounter a writing stumbling block and don't know how to move forward in their writing? How can they become writing problem solvers that cause the least amount of collateral damage to the writers around them?* and *How do we as teachers set up the way we manage meeting with students?* can lead to more time for writing and for meeting with kids.

We have stood on the shoulders of Gail Boushey and Joan Moser, "The Sisters." Their thinking, along with the work of Lucy Calkins, her amazing staff developers from the Teachers College Reading and Writing Project, and many other experts in writing instruction, guide us in developing ways to manage our classrooms during writing time. Our take on management is a culmination of all we have learned from the experts. When we look at what drives *our* success with being able to work with kids more frequently we see that it is based on the following:

- Routine
- Choice
- Organized Materials
- Partner Work

For us, these overarching goals are what we have found to help us engage with more kids, more often, in more meaningful ways. We now find ourselves being able to engage in conferences with less finger snapping at other children in the room, less stink eye to off-task kids, and less distraction in general. When kids have a consistent routine, choice within the routine, materials that are easy to find, and the chance to interact with others when necessary in appropriate ways, they are more on task, independent, and driven. Then we can get to the work of teaching.

ROUTINE

Ann Marie Corgill says it perfectly in her book *Of Primary Importance: What's Essential in Teaching Young Writers*: "The management work you do first will set the stage for what your young writers are capable of accomplishing throughout the year. Keep your strategy instruction simple at the beginning of the year, and teach your students ways to begin and sustain their writing work for days at a time" (2008, 79). It is essential to build routines in elementary classrooms, especially when it comes to writing. The children need the predictability of the structure to be able to focus on the task at hand. We have found that unpredictability plus young children usually equals chaos. Not a recipe for writing success. Look at your schedule and block off consistent time for writing. For Jen it is forty minutes before lunch four times a week. Kristin is able to pull together an hour most days. Jen just met a teacher who lamented that her schedule mandates only twenty minutes a day for her kindergartners. Not great, but something. Once you have established the days and time, guard them as best you can. We are teachers too, living in the world of field trips, holiday celebrations, surprise announcements, and assemblies, so we understand that uninterrupted time in the classroom is precious and worth fighting for.

Once you have a predictable time, think about how you want to teach your writers. Make sure you decide on a procedure for how writing time will go and keep it consistent. In our classrooms we use a writing workshop model. We start each workshop with a short strategy lesson that helps kids notice what writers do, then the kids move into independent writing time, followed by partner time to share and work on writing, and ending with a writer's share. (For more information on the writing workshop model look up the work being done by Lucy Calkins and her colleagues at the Teachers College Reading and Writing Project within Columbia University.) We strive for forty-five minutes to an hour of writing four days a week. Gail Boushey and Joan Moser include "Work on Writing" as part of their Daily 5 structure (Boushey and Moser 2014). Students are taught how to work on their writing as a choice during the literacy block, and that becomes the time set aside for this work each day. Whichever writing structure you use in your classroom, keep it consistent and reliable. The reward of having a predictable routine is that once routines are established, your writing lessons can focus on ways to help kids improve their writing instead of having to teach management lessons at the same time. Kids are able to learn one thing at a time, so keeping the focus on the writing lesson is the ultimate way to successfully transfer the strategy taught.

The predictability of structure and routine helps to simmer down kids at both ends of the "needing attention spectrum." There are the "Chihuahua" kids, whom our friends Joan Moser and Gail Boushey talk about in their workshops. These are the kids who are constantly at your side looking for attention and yipping, "When can we meet?" "Can I share my writing with you?" But there are also the quiet ones, who try to get by unnoticed and are too timid or reluctant to ask for help with their writing or hope you don't notice they haven't been writing at all. With a predictable structure, all the kids know they will be conferred with and the focus can get back on writing. Routine allows for writing and conferring to happen successfully, so be consistent even on the days you feel tired and unfocused, or don't think you have it in you. Once you set up a routine, stick with it.

Next we need to talk about how kids become independent within the routine. Since reading *The Daily 5: Fostering Literacy Independence in the Elementary Grades,* we have started using I-Charts and have not looked back. I-Charts (*I* stands for independence) are used to create independence among the students and hold them accountable for their choices within writing time. The chart is created by a class with the teacher's guidance. Behaviors that are expected get listed and the students practice the behaviors that will help them become better writers. For example, we might write on the chart, "Write the whole time." One student will model for the class what writing the whole time might look like and the teacher will ask the class, "Will this help you get better at writing?" The class will then discuss how writing the whole time builds stamina and the more you write, the better you will get. Then the same student who modeled the correct behavior will model it incorrectly and not write the whole time. The teacher will ask the question again about whether that kind of behavior will help them become better writers and they all laugh and say, "No!" The correct behavior will be modeled again and the students will then go off to try it on their own. Each behavior added to the I-Chart will follow the same routine. We continue to add strategies to the chart as we model expected behaviors with the whole group. Here are some of the other behaviors we list on our I-Charts:

- Stay in one spot.
- Keep your eyes on your writing.
- Be a problem solver if you get stuck.

In the beginning of the year, the teacher stays out of the way and lets the students practice the behavior independently with no guidance or support because the goal is self-monitoring. The teacher makes no eye contact with a student, does not walk around the room or give verbal reminders. Once the children's stamina for the behavior is at an end, writing time is over for the day so as not to model incorrect behavior. The students meet, reflect on how they did with the behaviors listed on the I-Chart, record the time spent writing successfully that day, and set a goal for beating the time the next day. The whole process is repeated each day until the students are monitoring themselves with no teacher support for an extended period of time. We aim for at least thirty minutes a day (longer for the older kids), and then finally we begin to confer. Integrating the I-Chart and practicing the expected behaviors right from the beginning of the school year sets the tone for how writing time will go and allows us to spend time conferring and not managing. You can find more specifics about using I-Charts in your classroom, the research that supports the work, and what to do with kids who struggle to self-monitor in *The Daily 5: Fostering Literacy Independence in the Elementary Grades* by Boushey and Moser (2014).

Jennifer Jacobson guarantees that "Once your class is successfully engaged in writer's workshop, you will insist on finding more time in your day for writing. And you'll know you've truly arrived when you gain an unexpected free moment and the kids shout, 'Can we write?'" (2010, 28).

We do have to brush up on our routine throughout the year. We often review expectations after long breaks, and if we notice that writers are not maintaining certain habits, we build in time to practice again. If we neglect to hold ourselves and our students accountable, our writing time can crumble. After the winter break Kristin noticed that Spencer was doing karate moves during writing, Sofia and Brynn were chatting about what they had done over the break, and Elena was following Kristin around the room. Kristin called the class back to the carpet, shared that they had a problem, quickly reviewed the expectations, and then sent the students off to practice. Kristin walked around to observe and make sure that all students were on task. On another day, Kristin noticed that supplies were low, so before teaching writing, she asked all writers to check their desks for any items that had not been returned. After most of the pens, highlighters, and scissors were returned, Kristin added in a few more items from her closet. By taking five or ten minutes to replenish the missing supplies,

Kristin was able to sit down to teach writing knowing that when she sent her writers off she could confer instead of running around hunting down supplies. Routine and practice is what gets us there.

CHOICE

How invested are you in a task of someone else's choosing? Jen loves to write as a hobby but agonized over every assigned paper she had to write for graduate school, because the topic was rarely a choice. Kristin loves planning and decorating for dinner gatherings at her home with friends, but when told she needed to plan someone else's bridal shower wasn't quite as invested.

As teachers, we see choice creating engagement in our own classrooms. If kids are engaged in the writing process we can spend more time meeting with kids individually and less time reacting to off-task behaviors. This is how choice falls under the heading of "Frequency" for us.

It was the end of the first-grade school year and the students in Jen's class had worked through many monthlong writing projects based on different genres. She was in the middle of a content-area unit on insects where the kids were observing insects, writing about insects, and reading about insects. Ants were busy creating tunnels in plastic anthills, ladybugs were emerging from their pupae, and butter-flies were hatching from their chrysalides. Could you imagine anything better in a first-grade classroom?

She had just sat down to start writing workshop when Hunter raised his hand. "I have this great idea for a book about an awesome knight and the adventures he has," he said. "Could we just write about what we want today instead of working on our insect projects?"

The school year was wrapping up in a few weeks and the kids really needed to finish their writing work on insects, but she could hear the earnest plea in his question and see others beginning to nod and whisper to each other about things they had in mind to write about that day, so she made one of those "in the mo-ment" teacher decisions that changes everything. "Let's do it," she said. "Today you can decide what you want to write about."

Eyes lit up with excitement. The questions began. "What can we write about?" they asked.

"Whatever is on your mind," she replied.

"Can we write with a friend?"

"If you think you can get writing done with a friend."

"What can we use to write? Where can we write?"

Her answer was the same: "Do what you want, as long as you are getting writing done."

Off they went. What happened next still gives us pause. As she watched them get settled, she realized this was no ordinary writing day. Instead of jumping in to confer, she decided to sit back and watch, really watch, what was happening. Kevin, Brody, and Kyle (whom she usually had to prod to get going) were already working on a play they wanted to perform for the class. Angelina and Samantha were reading to each other parts of what they had written and were helping each other make corrections, and Hunter was in a whole new world with his awesome knight. Everywhere she looked, each and every child was engaged, busy, and happily creating writing projects. The energy was electric, a busy hum of children focused and excited about what they were doing. All she could think was, "Wow, this is the power of choice at work!"

When Jen shared all the great things that were happening in her room because of choice, Kristin thought about trying it out in her class. However, as much as we are alike, we are also very different. Kristin is more of a control freak, so she was concerned that giving students choice meant she would lose control. Although Kristin wanted to offer more choice, she was really nervous about what would happen. But Kristin learned that she could continue to teach the qualities of good writing, and that writers could apply the strategies she taught in whatever genre they chose. She learned that choice is not about fluff. When planning for choice a teacher has to make sure she is grounded in something. Because we are grounded in teaching our kids the qualities of good writing, we are able to allow room for choice while still focusing on major goals.

Matt Glover, along with Lucy Calkins and her colleagues, have had a major impact on our thinking about choice in the classroom. Matt Glover tells us, "If we look at a typical student day and analyze how many true choices a student has each day, we see that in many classrooms children are presented with few options. Yet as educators we know that choice plays a major role in learning" (2009, 41). Knowing this, when we talk with Matt and other educators about different ways we can give kids choice in the classroom it comes down to the fact that opportunities for choice can exist within the writing part of the day. We can give kids choice and ownership over things like the following:

- Topic
- Genre
- Materials

Topic Choice

When students are allowed to choose their own topics to write about, engagement and stamina increase. Having to write to a prompt that you may or may not have any background knowledge for leads to less elaboration and voice, among other things. Consider a writing piece by a child about seeing their brand-new baby sister for the first time as opposed to the writing that would be produced from a prompt like, "Pretend you are the Easter Bunny; what would you put in the Easter baskets?" Which piece would you rather read—or write, for that matter? Professional writers get to think about and choose topics they are invested in; why not give the same opportunity to our kids?

Some of you might be thinking, "What about kids who say they have nothing to write about? Don't specific prompts help those kids?"

We argue that it may help the student begin, but the quality of the writing and the stamina for sticking with the piece through the processes of drafting and revising won't be as strong, nor will the student be as invested to work through the tougher parts of writing. The student who gets to write about things that matter to him or her is more likely to work through tricky parts to make sure the writing is the best it can be because the story matters and the student wants to share it. If you have a child who is stuck, instead of giving a specific prompt, consider teaching prompts that are more open-ended, such as the following:

- Think about a person you know and write a story about that person.
- Think about a place you've been and write a story about that place.
- Look at the books in the classroom and see what other writers are writing about. Could you write about the same thing?
- Is there something you know a lot about? Snakes, sharks, or gymnastics?
- Is there something you are really interested in?
- Think about different emotions to get an idea for writing. Your happiest moment, an embarrassing moment, a sad moment . . . You get the idea.

These prompts, created through our work with the Reading and Writing Project, don't force a writer into a topic he or she knows nothing about, but instead spark an idea for how to begin a personal journey into the writing process that is real and invested. If kids have strategies and prompt ideas that are internalized, they will be writing more and creating less distraction. This gives you the freedom to meet with more writers.

Some of you might now be thinking, "Well, what about test taking? Kids have to know how to write from prompts to take tests, right?"

It seems more and more teachers are spending the majority of their writing blocks across the entire year focusing only on writing prompts. We do agree that students need to score well on state writing tests so (depending on where you live) teachers can keep their jobs, schools can get money, schools can keep their rating, and teachers can earn bonuses or be recognized as outstanding teachers. We agree that kids need to be able to write from prompts on certain occasions but that is *not*, repeat *not*, the *only* kind of writing they should be exposed to. We take a month and teach prompt writing as a genre as one type of writing a writer may be called to do. During that month we may research all the different kinds of prompts that might be thrown at them and help them understand how to build a writing piece around the topic. The unit is filled with specific writing strategies to achieve this goal. So while we do understand the need for prompts, we try to give students as much topic choice as possible when we can. We have also found that by using the qualities of good writing, including how to generate ideas as a focus for writers from the very beginning of the school year, the students are prepared to write in any genre even with a prompt. We will discuss more about the qualities and generating ideas in Chapter 4. Let kids decide on topics as much as possible to increase engagement and decrease management issues.

Genre Choice

Another way we can give kids choice in writing is by letting them pick the genre in which they would like to write. If Jen's son, Will, could write only graphic novels and comics that is what he would do. Kids have specific genres they feel good about writing in, so anytime you can find the opportunity to offer genre as a choice you will also increase motivation just like we saw in Jen's room that May day.

In our classrooms, we spend a month or so at a time on a genre study but look for ways to include choice when we can. Jen begins the year with an inquiry unit based around how writers find ideas for writing, what materials writers use, who writers write for, and how writers write so others can read their work. This unit enables the children to write in any genre using the strategies acquired through the inquiry unit.

Kristin has developed a monthlong author study unit based on the writer Marissa Moss. Kristin chose Marissa Moss because she writes in a variety of genres (historical fiction, journaling, and picture books). She uses the qualities of good writing, but she also does interesting things with structure, elaboration, and voice and has a great website where young writers can learn about her writing process. Young writers can write in any genre using writing techniques they learn from Marissa Moss. Students learn about word choice, different fonts, paragraphing, imagery, and more. While students are learning skills they can implement them in fiction, comics, narratives, essays, and nonfiction.

FIGURE 3.1
Will's Comic, Inspired by Stephen McCranie's Mal and Chad Series

And yes, Jen's son, Will, did take the opportunity to write a comic during this unit (Figure 3.1) and loved every minute of it! Will had the opportunity to choose his genre but the accountability to apply the skills that he was taught. As hard as it is for some of us (Kristin) to let go, it is empowering for the writer. Kristin is amazed every year at the transformation in her classroom when she offers choice. The kids who typically procrastinate, ask to go to the bathroom, or socialize are engaged, productive, and excited.

So even if you can't give your students a choice in genre throughout the entire year, see if you can find interesting ways to break a genre down into more specific subsets that can infuse choice. For example, Kristin teaches a nonfiction unit where she allows her students to choose the *type* of informational text they create. Students can choose from traditional nonfiction books, narrative nonfiction books, question-and-answer books, or pattern nonfiction books. This gives her the ability to include choice even when the genre is predetermined.

Choice of Materials

Another way we can give students choice during writing time is with writing materials. Pencil or pen? Quick sketches or illustrations with markers? Paper choice is a huge one. One of the benefits of starting the year with an inquiry unit on what writers need is that Jen was able to create different paper choices for the kids based on what kids notice in books around them in the classroom. Jen had the kids partner up and look through many different types of books in the classroom and then sketch the kind of paper that they felt could help them write like that author. For instance, Sophia and Kai noticed that their book had a picture under the words instead of at the top of the page, so they asked for paper with a picture box at the bottom of the page instead, with lines above it. Sammy and Hanna noticed that there were sentences placed next to different pictures on a page so they drew a sketch of paper Jen could type up to emulate that format. Dasha and Lindy loved the fact that some books had text that was only in speech bubbles

so they asked for that. Figures 3.2, 3.3, and 3.4 show some of the different paper choices the kids came up with that were then put on the writing shelf to be used. With older students Kristin offers notebook paper and white copy paper. Some students write while others type.

Even though choice in materials seems like a small thing, it is another way to engage the students in our classroom. The more choices we give, the more likely they are to be engaged and motivated to write, and the more we can meet with writers without distraction. As Matt Glover reminds us, "When a child has a choice, he has some degree of control over the learning experience" (2009, 41). When kids feel in control of what is happening, they are not only focused but emotionally ready for the tasks at hand. This leads to the kind of engagement we need to be able to focus our attention on writing and writers and not on managing the classroom environment. So ask yourself, what kinds of choices, big or small, could you provide for the students in your classroom during writing time?

FIGURE 3.2
Paper for Writing and an Illustration

FIGURE 3.3
Paper for Writing with Speech Bubbles and an Illustration

ORGANIZED MATERIALS

How many times during writing time do you get interrupted by a student while conferring only to hear, "My pencil broke!" or "I can't find a blue marker!" This can get frustrating really quickly and interrupt the good work you are trying to do with the student you are conferring with. Having a plan for writing materials ahead of time leads to less problem solving and more conferring time. We want you to be able to use the time you have for working with writers, not finding a new tape roll.

Student Materials

The materials we use for writing are organized and kept in the same place all year long. The materials are clearly labeled and the "job" of each one is explained at the beginning of the year when we introduce "writer's tools." Just as artists need

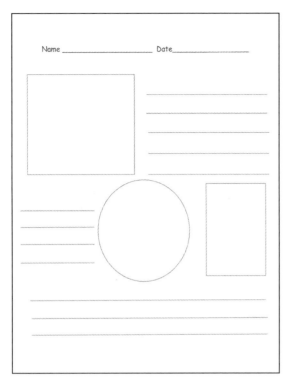

FIGURE 3.4
Paper for Multiple Illustrations and Labels (Often Used for
Informational Writing)

paints, brushes, and a canvas or electricians need wire, pliers, and splitters, writers
need tools. We have a place in the classroom where the writing materials are kept.
Jen has a shelf in her first-grade classroom for pens, pencils, paper, writing folders,
and student supply baskets (Figure 3.5). Kristin keeps her student writing supplies
on top of a low filing cabinet next to her writing workshop carpet (Figure 3.6).
Kristin does not have a lot of wall space, so she uses a large window to post her
writing skills and the windowsill to hold her reference books and mentor texts.
Here is where we bend and say, go to Pinterest right away. In this case, someone
more savvy than all of us has created labels that will match your decor exactly so
you don't have to spend precious time on that. We also have to teach our writers
how to use our classroom devices to research when we are writing informational
pieces. Students need to know how to navigate websites, videos, webcams, and

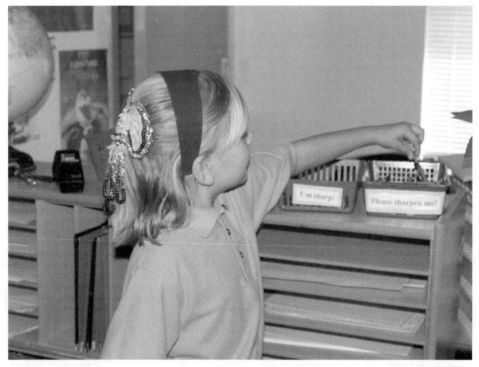

FIGURE 3.5
Jen's Materials

virtual tours. Older students also need to know how to type when they are ready
to use computers to type their drafts.

We also have to have a plan for the upkeep of writing tools. Not every material
is returned every day and, well, we aren't always sure what happens to the pens
and pencils in our rooms, but it can feel like the kids are eating them at the rate
they disappear. So, it is important to have a plan for replenishing the supplies and
keeping them organized. It can be a job you add to your job chart, or it could be
a task for one of your students who arrives in class early, or it might be easier for
you to just double-check the supplies before or after school. Kristin often has her
students empty out their desks when the scissors or the tape have gone missing
and after a five-minute class cleanup, most of the writing materials are returned.

We spend the first month of school talking about the writing tools in the classroom and what they are used for when writing. Jen made the mistake one year
of putting everything on the shelf at the beginning of the school year, believing

(foolishly) the kids would just be able to figure out how to use the materials appropriately. After a week of marker tattoos up and down their arms, tape rings on their fingers, and a book with fifty (no lie—fifty) staples used, it became obvious that kids need a little teensy-weensy more guidance. So now, we introduce writing tools as they are needed and with explicit modeling.

> Jen: *Boys and girls, today we are going to start thinking about ways that writers can add more to their books. If you found that you have more to say on a page, but the page is full, you can add a flap of paper to the side or bottom to add more. To do this you will have to use a tool that writers use called tape.*

At this point, Jen would model how to appropriately use the tape to add a flap of paper to add more detail to a section of writing.

FIGURE 3.6
Kristin's Materials

Jen: *See how I pull off just enough to hold the paper in place? If I pull too much, there is too much tape and it all sticks to itself. [Pulls too much and gets tape stuck all over her hands.] Yikes, this won't work, and if I waste the tape there won't be any left for other kids. If I use too small a piece, the flap won't stay on for long. I need a piece that is just right. This is how a writer uses a writer's tool.*

It may seem silly to spend the time going over something so simple but in the end it saves us from having to say sarcastic things like, "Have you lost your mind?" when you find a child's book (or arm) covered in tape instead of being able to focus on kids and their writing. To read more about student materials and what to use we recommend Jennifer Jacobson's book *No More "I'm Done!" Fostering Independent Writers in the Primary Grades* (2010). Jennifer has a great chapter describing how to support student independence with organized and ready writing materials.

With older writers we can move through how to use writing tools a lot faster; however, we spend more time and energy reinforcing how they will spend their writing time. Older writers still need to be reminded how to use writing tools, but they also need very clear boundaries so that they do not spend their time socializing, practicing their pencil drumming, or performing karate moves. It is a mistake to think that older students do not need to practice routines and procedures, even with something as simple as materials. Older students can easily get lost in jockeying for their social standing, entertaining a buddy, and if love is in the air . . . well, good luck without clear expectations!

Organized Teacher Materials

Now that you have the kids organized, you need to get yourself ready. We all have those days where you just get the kids settled with their writing pieces, the Pandora spa music calms in the background, and you are ready to get to work. Then you realize you haven't fired up the computer (if that is how you take notes), or you can't find the writing piece you wanted to use in a conference, or you can't find the conferring notebook you had just five minutes ago and now you are feeling flustered. Or you have all of that, you sit down to work with a student, and you realize you need to grab a book from across the room to show them a great lead, or you need a sticky note from the other side of the classroom and the conferring session gets totally stalled while you are looking for supplies.

It is not just the writing materials for the kids that need to be in place to keep the conferring momentum going. The materials you use as a teacher need to be organized as well. When you have your conferring notes organized and accessible, your writing models in hand in case they are needed to illustrate a strategy, and your pencil behind your ear, you can conduct a conferring session with a student with ease and less distraction. This allows you more time to meet with more kids.

Before you begin conferring during writing time you are going to want to make sure you have the following things pulled together in a kit and ready to travel:

1. Conferring notes—either on paper or on the computer

2. Pencil/revision pen

3. Writing examples

4. Sticky notes

There are all kinds of ways you can record notes on the kids you work with. We have pretty much tried every version imaginable. We started with a separate notebook for each child so that we could keep all of our notes for a student's reading and writing in one place. This worked until we had to do progress reports and had to tote around twenty notebooks. Then we moved to sticky notes, with the hope that the little notes would keep their stick long enough to end up in the child's file folder on the other side of the room. Even the "super sticky" notes didn't stick throughout the year. We ended up losing the sticky notes and the notes we needed written on them. Next we tried keeping notes for all students on a one-page grid, with each child getting a separate box in the grid. The goal was to meet with each child at least once a week (as evidenced by the filled-in boxes) and then file the week's grid in a binder. The problem was we started a new, blank grid page each week and never remembered what we had done with each child the previous week. It was hard to track one child's progress across time, because the notes were on different sheets of paper. We were not consistently teaching toward a specific goal. Then we read *The CAFE Book: Engaging All Students in Daily Literacy Assessment and Instruction* (Boushey and Moser 2009) and found great success using the conferring sheets from the back of the book. Each child now has his or her own sheet with overall writing goals at the top and a place to record teaching points and next steps. There is also a place to assess the use of the skill from conference to conference. Jen maintains a separate orange folder for each of her students. (She uses blue folders for notes on their reading so she can easily grab the right folder as needed.) Each orange folder has that student's conferring sheet stapled on one side, and Jen keeps all of that student's assessment pieces inside the folder for easy reference. She keeps all the orange folders in a file box lying on its side. She grabs the folder on top at the start of each writing workshop and confers with that student first. After conferring, she puts that student's folder at the bottom of the pile in the file box, takes the next folder from the top, and continues the process. This helps ensure she meets with all the kids consistently through the week and doesn't inadvertently forget to check in with a child. Of course there are times when she might meet with one child twice before meeting with another child because of where that child might be in writing. For the most part, rotating the folders helps ensure that even the quiet writers get some teacher time.

Kristin has loved using Gail and Joan's Pensieve binder system and now uses their online system. The online version of this note-taking system is called the CCPensieve. There is a small fee (it is *so* worth the fee!) to access the CCPensieve, but the organizing and note-taking options are endless and they are improving it every day. Check it out at ccpensieve.com. We have found that it fits perfectly with the writing format we will be discussing in this book. If you don't have the funds on your huge teacher's salary to purchase an online note-taking system you can also consider Evernote. This is a great free app that lets you take notes on students and even holds pictures and audio so you can take pictures of a child's work or record audio conference notes and add them to a child's folder.

Whatever you decide works best for you, make sure you have an organized way to take notes on your work with each child to help you plan next steps for formative assessment. We will talk more about how we assess our writers in Chapter 5.

We also make sure to have writing examples with us and ready to go. If we are focusing on leads, we will bring mentor texts with us that show examples of strong leads. If we are working on descriptive language, we have examples of that. We use both student work and published picture books as models. We also use our own writing pieces created during mini-lessons to illustrate strategies. Jen keeps all the student assessment writing in the folders she has for each child. (We have the students complete an on-demand writing assessment at the end of each unit; see Chapter 5, "Follow-Up: Making Our Teaching Stick.") This way she can look for evidence (or lack of evidence) of a strategy being used across pieces. She also uses the pieces to remind students how they used strategies or writing craft in other places in their writing.

We use sticky notes because we are proponents of not writing on student drafts. Marking up a student's paper takes away the ownership of his or her work and also focuses on what is going wrong. We use the sticky notes to remind students of a strategy or to show a student examples of the strategy we are trying to teach. The student can then keep the sticky note in his or her writing folder to refer to.

PARTNER TIME

Let's be honest: having kids work together as writing partners can be really productive or it can be a total waste of time, to say nothing of being a management nightmare. The most obvious reason is that when you ask young kids to talk, talk they will. The problem is that the talk is not always about writing and can become very distracting to all involved. What we have learned is that writers need to talk through their writing and to hear it read out loud to know what it really says, and we cannot meet with individual kids often enough to get that kind of talk done well. We can increase the frequency with which we meet with kids to confer if we employ another way for kids to share so they aren't constantly coming to us creating distraction—partner time.

Partnerships can play many roles. Partners can share with each other for the pleasure of sharing their writing, partners can work on helping each other, and partners can work together toward a common goal.

A lot of young writers get so excited about what they have written that they are dying to share right then and there. We have had many kids over the years say things like, "PLEASE, just read it really quick!" not only when we are trying to confer with another child but even as we are walking to lunch or packing up for the day. Writers want to share, and having a partner ready to listen provides that outlet so we don't have to fill the role 100 percent of the time.

Besides sharing their work, partners can help each other. It is common for writers to think that their writing is very clear because they have background knowledge, personal experience, or a lot of research swimming around in their brain when they are writing. When a writer attempts to reread and revise, it can be really challenging to decipher what is on paper and what is still in the writer's mind. That is where a partner can be really helpful. A partner can listen to the writer read what they have and ask questions or make suggestions when they get confused or lost or want to know more. Jen saw this with Lila, who was sharing a fiction piece about a princess whose hair kept changing colors in the picture but she never mentioned it in the story. When her partner asked her about the ever-changing hair, Lila told her partner, "That is the problem in the story, the princess's hair keeps changing colors!" to which her partner responded, "Ooh, I was just confused because you never said that in your words." Jen watched Lila flip through the pages and realize that she thought she had written it, but hadn't. Lila was able to go back into her story and make her words match the pictures. This is just one of many examples of how being able to read work aloud helps a writer revise.

Writers can also use a partner to work toward a common goal. When we teach informational writing there is often a lot of research involved. When Kristin's students study marine life she often has several writers interested in learning about the same creature. When this happens, she allows them to share what they are learning with each other. One morning Atticus was reading an article about narwhals, and when he learned that narwhals could grow two horns, he grabbed Henry to show him the article. Both writers documented the article in their bibliography, talked about what they learned, and then went back to researching independently. Sofia and Meriel shared headphones and watched videos about how dolphins are captured and purchased for theme parks. The video was so shocking that the girls couldn't help but share what they were thinking. Sofia and Meriel would pause the video when they learned something new or wanted to talk through what they viewed to process the shocking information. Evan and Grayson were tackling complex text because they wanted to learn more about how people are harming whales. They often stopped to talk through a paragraph and take notes before moving forward. Sounds great, right?

This can be easier said than done. Ruth Ayres and Stacey Shubitz write, "When it comes to hitches in writing workshop, peer conferring seems to be at the top of the list. Because writers in our classroom are amateurs, it makes sense that they won't offer sophisticated advice to one another" but then go on to say, "Peer conferring should be more about the process of talking to other writers and less about the outcome. Talking with others is a worthy way to spend time as writers" (2010, 202). Take the pressure off. We can't expect young children to "teach" each other as well as we can when conferring with them, but just being able to hear their words out loud, or to have someone listen and ask authentic questions about what was written, or finally, to work toward a common goal can be enough to satisfy the needs of a writer.

Knowing that writing talk is important to writers and creates less distraction for the teacher if put into place correctly, the question remains, how do we navigate this "sticky" part of our writing time?

First, we know that young children aren't naturally collaborative. Watch any group of children trying to play a game of soccer at recess with no official referee to see that point illustrated perfectly. We have to do what Ayres and Shubitz recommend: "Before any other skills [for peer conferring] can be taught, a culture of encouragement and support ought to be established. This structure is too important to be left in fate's hands" (2010, 202). Students need to see what respect and encouragement look like while working with another writer. We model this explicitly during our writing shares (which we explore in Chapter 5) by having children watch us give writers compliments and suggestions and by teaching them how to give compliments and appropriate feedback in a whole-group setting so we are all hearing it together. We have the kids pay attention to the tone of our voice—not only what we are saying to the writer but how we are saying it. We set up a classroom environment where we, as the teachers, model patience and respect in the way we talk to the students throughout the entire day. We try very hard not to call out students in front of the whole class but rather speak to them privately so everyone knows they learn in a place where they won't be embarrassed or ridiculed in front of their peers. We try very hard not to use sarcasm with students but rather model supportive and kind words. We try to create a safe environment for learning and sharing. We do all these things to set a tone of encouragement before we ask kids to share their writing with another person. We also begin the year with activities that center on listening. We create opportunities for kids to have to listen to each other and respond to what their partner has said. At the beginning of the school year, Jen has her first graders sit across from a partner and practice having one partner tell something about himself, such as what his favorite hobby is, and then have the second partner repeat what she heard. From there they move on to repeating what they heard, then adding something on the same topic. For example, "You said that you like to ride your bike. I like to ride my bike too. I ride it with my brother in the neighborhood." Such a simple exercise helps children understand that listening is a skill that needs to be taught for any kind of real work to get done.

Second, we have more success teaching our writers how to work with partners if we introduce ongoing strategies at the beginning of the year. Kristin takes videos of her students while they meet and then they watch the videos as a class to determine what is going well and what needs some adjusting. After analyzing videos, her class comes up with I-Charts that have statements like the following:

1. I will look my partner in the eye.

2. I will sit next to my partner.

3. I will listen to my partner.

4. I will offer a compliment.

5. I will try to help.

6. I will stay on task.

The charts are kept up all year and reviewed as partnership work needs tweaking. We may also have the kids sit in a circle with two partners in the middle and have the kids watch the partnership talk about their writing together while following the suggestions on the I-Charts. Because partnerships do require frequent maintenance, when we plan units we often weave in small amounts of time to remind partners what we expect and how they can work together productively. Here are some things we might say:

"Don't forget to sit side by side and use eye contact or nod your head to let your partner know you are listening when he is sharing."

"You can share interesting research with your partner but make sure you both jot down the source in your bibliography."

"Make sure to ask you partner if he or she wants to share his or her writing or is looking for feedback!"

Third, choosing partnerships can be a work in progress. Productive partnerships take time, so we try to choose partners wisely at the beginning of the year and prefer to keep partners together throughout the year unless we notice there is a problem. It takes time to build trust, honesty, and security so that, ideally, two students will stay together. However, we do not hesitate to end a partnership if two students just can't stay on task. We often adjust when students move, have squabbles that they can't shake, or we gain new students. If we give kids a choice of partner, we take the advice of Colleen Cruz, who tells her fourth-grade students, "Finally, I reserve the right to dissolve a partnership and move partners if I think they will not work well together. So do not make the mistake of choosing somebody simply because he or she is your friend. Choose someone you can work with" (2004, 112). By giving ownership and choice coupled with accountability, many partnerships work well.

Fourth, think about the logistics of how you will have partners share to minimize disruption. We have everyone meet with their partners at the same time. That way, everyone in the classroom is basically talking at the same time so we don't have to worry about kids becoming distracted and not getting writing done. Other teachers designate places in the classroom for partners to meet away from quiet areas in the room where kids are trying to concentrate on their pieces. Ayres and Shubitz recommend that a teacher "Identify three places in the classroom where peer conferring is expected. This allows students who prefer quiet when writing to avoid these spots. It also allows for only three peer conferences to occur at a given time. If all the spaces are filled and two students want to have a conference, they need to wait until a space opens" (2010, 209).

When we let the kids take on the "talking it out" work for us, the time we spend during writing time is left for the more important job of meeting with kids to support them one-on-one.

Once kids are engaged and independent during writing time and we have started meeting with kids more frequently, the next step to think about is how to focus our conferences with each student to help make the most growth in a short amount of time. This brings us to the second F: Focus.

CHAPTER 4

FOCUS: KEEPING SPECIFIC GOALS IN MIND

The fire drill is about to start, you just got an e-mail about an after-school meeting, Rebecca says her thumb hurts, Sally is crying because Megan just said she is not her best friend anymore, and Jameel just wants to go home and play on his Xbox. And you're supposed to be teaching . . . Sound familiar?

If we can't control much, we at least want to be able to control how we approach conferences with writers to make the instruction as focused and clear as possible. As we brainstormed the what and how of our writing instruction we found ourselves struggling with the same questions contributing to lack of focus:

"What is essential to teach kids about writing?"

"Are there specific foundational strategies I should be teaching them? What are they?"

"When the charts come down at the end of each unit, why does it feel like the strategies get retired along with them?"

"When I confer with kids in writing I feel like I don't have a plan. A lot of times my suggestions are genre based and I am just teaching to whatever they are writing that day. What should I focus on to help the writer improve no matter what genre we are working on?"

Because our questions really reflected the disorganization of our teaching, we made it our goal to find a way to organize and focus our own minds so that we could teach more effectively. When we sat down to figure out how to become better teachers of writing, these fundamental questions guided us to the central idea of focus. These questions were really about how to focus writing instruction on the strategies that would matter most to the writers in our classrooms.

As mentioned in the introduction we chose five qualities that we believe are basic elements that good writing is built on. Educators differ in their opinions of what the qualities of good writing are (Routman 2005; Culham 2005; Graves and Kittle 2005; Calkins 2013). We have found that what matters most in the crafting of writing is structure, conventions, focus, voice, and elaboration. These qualities of good writing are used in all genres of writing and provide clear goals for instruction.

In *The CAFE Book: Engaging All Students in Daily Literacy Assessment and Instruction*, Gail Boushey and Joan Moser center their work on comprehension, accuracy, fluency, and expanding vocabulary as overarching goals for reading instruction. Their ideas changed the way we conferred with kids in reading. Once we set these reading goals for our kids, the focus of our reading conferences became clearer to both of us and to our students. The strategies we taught to reach those goals informed our teaching decisions and our kids grew as readers. With Boushey and Moser's CAFE book as our inspiration, we decided that we would begin to focus our writing instruction like they did with their reading instruction—on the overarching goals that good writers use. We realized that the only way writing strategies could transfer from one unit to the next or one genre to the next was going to be to focus on these overarching goals of good writing. Writers, for instance, use strategies for integrating voice into their writing no matter what genre they write in. Similarly, writers need to use strategies for creating focus in their writing no matter what genre. Once we realized we could use our qualities of good writing to inform our instruction, we never looked back.

Our hope was also to come up with a plan to make conferences less scattered and more focused. We wanted to stop bouncing from one strategy to the next with no clear idea of how to help each child improve as a writer, not just improve the piece of writing. The qualities of good writing help us keep a focus on the strategies we can use to help a writer succeed in one area before jumping to the next one. The biggest shift in our classrooms is in how we organize our thinking and instruction, not the actual instruction itself. Regardless of the curriculum you have been given, you can teach in a logical and purposeful way. We adjusted *how* we teach more than *what* we teach but the *how* has had a huge impact on the everyday transfer of the *what*. Most teachers are given a writing curriculum (the *what* that they teach) and that curriculum specifies what writing strategies should be taught. The problem is that most curriculums do not explain *how* to teach those strategies or what comes next after one strategy has been taught. We needed a clear direction, a bigger picture. We wanted to know how the everyday strategies we were teaching would fit into a broader goal of improving the overall writing that a writer produces. When we teach our writers with focus and frequency, and we follow up using the qualities of good writing, we are using our given curriculum *and* we are teaching with clarity.

We now focus on one goal until we start to see mastery. We go into conferences with a clear plan instead of winging it. We used to sit down with a writer, look at his writing, and hope that something intelligent would come to mind. Now, we sit down with a writer, look at our notes on our previous conference, and continue to coach the writer toward a goal, or we move on to a new goal if we see evidence that the writer is ready to move on. Like any teachers of young children, we love acronyms! Using *The CAFE Book* as our inspiration, we could see that kids hold on to learning when it is easily rememberable. Knowing this matters, we came up with the acronym I SCORE.

I   Ideas

S   Structure

C   Conventions

O   One Focus

R   Real Voice

E   Elaboration

When we talk to the kids at the beginning of the year about I SCORE, we tell them that these are the qualities that all good writers use in their writing. Earlier we discussed five qualities of good writing. We added a sixth, ideas, after realizing that most of our writers have the most trouble just coming up with something to write about. Without an idea, there is no writing to work on. This is why we teach specific strategies that writers use to come up with writing topics. We talk about how students will grow as writers if they have these as goals as they write. We make sure they know that all our thinking about writing this year will be based on these big goals. When you want to score in a soccer game, you have to use all the skills and strategies your coach teaches you, and the same goes for writing. We remind them how lucky they are that as writers they really only have six goals to help them "score" in writing. That is doable.

We keep these six goals in mind when we are teaching whole groups, small groups, and individuals. These goals guide us in the strategies we choose to introduce to kids. When we begin a unit, we look to see what our unit goals are and how I SCORE fits within a genre. We then tailor our strategies to fit these goals. Figure 4.1 shows an example of how Kristin plans a unit for her third graders using the I SCORE acronym with the qualities of good writing in mind. At the beginning of a new writing unit, she looks at the writing goals set by the mandated writing curriculum for our school and organizes them under the quality heading where each goal best fits. This reinforces the idea of focusing on broader goals and reminds her to be explicit when teaching, no matter what the group size is, and let the students know that the strategy will help them toward a bigger goal of writing. This drive toward broader goals clarifies writing for the students. They understand that each mini-lesson does not stand alone. They can see that every lesson we teach now falls under one of the six I SCORE goals we have set for our writers and feels organized and doable.

We keep these six I SCORE goals posted on the wall year-round and add strategies as the school year progresses. This growing chart holds our thinking and eliminates the problem we once had of kids not employing the writing strategies taught once a unit chart came down. Now the strategies stay up all year as a reminder to be used.

In the sections that follow, we illustrate how we use the qualities of good writing to focus our writing instruction, define each quality, describe the strategies we use to help students reach the goal or quality being taught, and offer examples of conferences with students around that quality. We integrate the Common Core standards covered in our teaching for those of you who are mandated to document their use in your own teaching. This focus on the qualities of good writing has changed the way we teach writing and has enabled our young writers to make the

Planning a Writing Unit: Nonfiction Unit
Lining up mini lessons according to the qualities of good writing:

Ideas:
1.heart mapping
2. I know/I wonder chart

Structure:
1.introductions
2. table of contents
3. topic sentences
4. paragraphs
5. headings and subheadings
6. Multiple fonts (this can be done as a quick mid workshop interruption bc I have already taught it)

Conventions:
1. capitals (beginning of a sentence, proper nouns, titles, chapters or headings)
2. ending punctuation
3.commas in a series
4. complete sentences
5.

Focus:
1. one topic
2. writes factual information (this is really taught during the research phase so I will remind during writing but don't need a full lesson

Voice:
1.Talk with a teaching voice (model with mentor text and students -Will, Robby, and Krish)
2. Did you know bubbles

Elaboration:
1. comparisons
2. captions and pictures
3. Diagrams, charts, maps, etc
4. content specific words
5. twin sentences

FIGURE 4.1

Planning a Nonfiction Writing Unit Using I SCORE

writing strategies they learn part of their writer's arsenal of tools. We hope the same will apply to you and the students you teach. Now, let's get focused!

IDEAS

We believe it is essential to teach writers how to get "good-fit" ideas for writing. Ideas rarely pop into our heads at just the right moment. Writing is a skill, and coming up with ideas for what to write about is a practiced skill as well. We use the term *good fit* with our students because we want them to learn that not every idea works. Students need to learn not only how to generate ideas but also, once they have come up with a list, how to decide which idea is the best one to focus on and develop. When given the tools and opportunity to practice this skill, writers can confidently begin a new draft in any genre.

We both bought in to the misconception that a person is born with the gift of writing when actually it is a practiced skill. The National Council of Teachers of English (NCTE) states that "everyone has the capacity to write; writing can be taught; and teachers can help students become better writers" (NCTE 2016). If we teach our students the first skill—how to come up with ideas—we can allow them to practice the skill of writing. This is often the biggest hurdle for beginning writers; they can quickly become frustrated and want to give up. As teachers, we need to model this step and share our own frustrations as we struggle for the right idea. Writers generate a lot of ideas; however, they choose only a few to draft. This is like throwing spaghetti on the wall to see what sticks. We also have to teach our students how to try out or rehearse ideas in order to discern which idea is the best one.

When choosing a topic for a nonfiction piece, Evan, a third grader, began with the idea of writing about whales. After generating ideas about what he knew about whales, he began to realize that what he really cared about was the fact that whales are becoming endangered. Instead of writing about everything he knew, he chose the idea he was most passionate about and was able to stay engaged in the writing piece throughout the whole unit. This is the first opportunity that writers have to revise in easy, nonthreatening ways. In third through fifth grades, when a writer commits to the wrong piece, they often struggle to elaborate and the piece often just fizzles out. When asked what the heart of the draft is, kids usually do not have an answer. Choosing the wrong topic is frustrating and time-consuming. Writers will spend a few days generating ideas and trying them out by talking them out, acting them out, making time lines or a table of contents, or sketching pictures. We then cut, change, or adjust what is not working, just like Evan was able to do when he realized that the endangerment of whales was what he really wanted to learn more about and teach to others. All this work makes the drafting process much easier. Evan did not have pages of writing before realizing the true focus of his book. Instead, Evan spent time creating heart maps, a prewriting strategy described by Georgia Heard (1999). He first jotted down all the reasons he really was interested in researching whales and took time to ponder why he cared about whales, what he loved about whales. After listing all the reasons he was interested and why he cared, Evan circled the one thought that was at the heart of his interest. He circled his note about how humans harm whales. He was able to narrow down what really interested him and then move forward, researching with a clear focus. For younger students, who are basically creating a new piece of writing every day, being able to independently come up with ideas for writing is an important and effective way to build writing stamina.

What Does the Common Core Say About Generating Ideas?
In our research of the Common Core State Standards (CCSS), we couldn't find any standard specifically saying that students should be able to come up with their own ideas for writing. Terms such as *write*, *narrate*, and *compose* are used, but there is nothing indicating that students should be able to come up with their own topics for writing independently.

So for a moment, we digress to two major points that we feel need to be mentioned. One point is that as educators, we always need to remember that the CCSS are a composition of skills sets deemed most important, but they are not an execution plan. The second point is that choice is a huge motivating factor in building stamina as a writer. If we give students choice in the topics they write about, then we can keep them engaged and motivated.

When we talk about the definition of ideas in our classrooms, we tell the kids that ideas mean topics they can come up with to write about each and every day.

Here is a list of strategies we share throughout the year and within writing units to help kids come up with their own ideas for writing:

- Look at pictures on your writing folder.
- Think of a person you know and things you have done with that person.

- Think of a place and things you have done at that place.
- Look at what your peers are writing about.
- Look at mentor texts and try out what other writers write about.
- Think of the first time you did something.
- Think of the last time you did something.
- Remember a time when you felt a strong emotion—excitement, disappointment, sorrow.
- Create a heart map (Heard 1999).

What Does Using Idea Strategies Successfully Look Like?

When you walk into a classroom where writers are generating ideas, you might see several students jotting down ideas in a notebook. Other writers are drawing quick sketches to think through a beginning, middle, and end. Some writers are talking to themselves or to a partner while other writers might be working on a story arc or a table of contents. You will often see writers gazing off because they are thinking. We encourage writers to choose ideas thoughtfully, which means they need time to think. Pencils are usually not flying across a page at this stage and that is normal.

What Should You Know Before Teaching Writers How to Come Up with Ideas?

Giving kids strategies for coming up with good-fit idea choices is something we do as a whole group for the first few weeks of school and are typically the strategies we teach first on the I SCORE chart. In order to work on the other goals, there has to be writing. Teaching the kids ways to be independent during writing time is the only way to move them forward as writers and also to ensure that we will be able to meet with everyone in small groups and one-on-one. Once we have added a few different strategies for coming up with ideas with the whole group, we can meet one-on-one with the kids who are still struggling to come up with ideas.

In his book *When Writing Workshop Isn't Working: Answers to Ten Tough Questions, Grades 2–5* (2005), Mark Overmeyer reminds us that when kids still struggle to come up with ideas it can be because we haven't given them a topic that is focused enough. We are proponents of giving kids choice in their writing, but that choice can still happen even if we narrow down the topic ideas for kids who struggle. As Overmeyer says, "If students are asked to write about their summer, or their favorite vacation, or even a birthday party, the problem is not that there is not enough to write about, but that there is still too much" (2005, 21–22). Not every writer gets overwhelmed in this way, but there are some children who will think of every birthday party they have ever been to and not be able to narrow it down. Then once a specific party is chosen there are many more options. Should I talk about the food or the presents? Should I write about how we picked the place to have the party? You should have a plan if you find that kids are still overwhelmed after you've given the whole group suggestions. Mark suggests that we encourage these kids to come up with a title that is more specific. Instead of writing about going to the Magic Kingdom, perhaps the child could title his piece "My Scary Time on Space Mountain." This not only gets him right into a specific story but will make it easier for him to elaborate and less likely that he will merely list events.

When you walk into our classrooms during writing time you will typically see many kids with their heads down, pencils in hand, drawing, writing, and creating with no teacher input whatsoever. You will also see two or three kids at any given time with their heads down on their desks, walking toward the bathroom door or drinking fountain, or using a pencil as a Star Wars light saber—along with many other writing avoidance techniques. These are the kids who need to strengthen their ability to come up with ideas for writing independently. Once kids get started with pencil to paper, we rarely have to intervene because stamina automatically comes with a good-fit topic choice. Kids who are avoiding writing can be pulled into a small group to relearn a strategy for how writers come up with ideas to get them going.

What Might Conferences That Teach Ways to Come Up with Ideas Look Like?

Pull up a (tiny) chair and join us in our classrooms as we teach some of these idea strategies to our young writers.

Jen walks over to Parker, a first grader in her classroom. He is the perfect example of a child who has trouble coming up with ideas for writing.

"Hey, Park, how is your writing going today?" She has already noticed the empty page and his focus, at this point, on how to flip a pencil so it lands just the way it started.

Parker's big brown eyes look at her and he says, "I don't know what to write about." After doing this kind of work for over ten years and having a good relationship with Parker, Jen has realized that there can be many different explanations for that statement. It could mean, "I stayed up too late last night so I am feeling too tired to write or do anything in particular.'" It could mean, "'Writing is hard for me and I would rather not put in the energy to do it right now." It could also mean, "I just don't have any ideas for writing." It is important for Jen to ask Parker so he can say in his own words what the hang-up is, instead of just assuming what it could be.

"Tell me more," Jen says casually.

"I can't think of an idea of what I want to write," admits Parker. Okay. Now she has narrowed it down. No assumptions made.

"That can be really frustrating. The same thing happens to me from time to time," admits Jen. Right here, it is important to note that because Jen is actually a writer herself, there is true empathy. She finds herself many times having the same problems the kids have and has brainstormed ways to get over those hurdles. If Jen wasn't a writer herself, it would be difficult to truly understand writing struggles and she would probably appear inauthentic to the kids.

"It does?" asks Parker. This time with a little bit of curiosity and interest.

"Yes, I write articles for teachers every month and sometimes I find myself just where you are right now. A blank piece of paper and no thoughts to write down. That can be hard. I do have a few tricks that I use and I was hoping I could show you one of them today to help get you started. Would that be okay?"

Reluctantly Parker says, "Okay." Although we all know that pencil flipping is a heck of a lot more fun!

"Okay, Park. One thing I do when I don't know what to write about is think of a person I know. Once I have that person in my head, I try to come up with three different things I have done with that person. When I think of a story, I put up a finger. When I have three fingers up, I ask myself, what story would I like to write today?"

Jen goes on, "Watch me, buddy. Then you can give it a try.

"I am thinking of my daughter, Caroline. Hmm . . . The first story I am think-ing of is when we went to a farm and she didn't want to go on the pony ride." Jen puts up one finger. "Now I am thinking of the time that Caroline fell at the drinking fountain and chipped her tooth. She really scared me." Jen puts up a second finger. "The third story is a funny one. I am thinking about the time that Caroline was singing the *Frozen* song all crazy and wrong in the backseat of my car and her big brother was yelling at her to stop hurting his ears.

"I guess out of all three stories the one about Caroline singing is the one I would like to write about most because it is a funny story and I like to write funny stories!

"Okay, Parker, now you give it a try. Think of someone you know," Jen says enthusiastically.

Parker chooses his friend Caleb and goes on to tell Jen three different times he has been with Caleb. He decides to write about the time he went to Caleb's house for a sleepover. Figure 4.2 shows the piece he ultimately came up with.

It should be noted that Parker would get stuck a lot over the year. In fact, his goal for the first few months of school was ideas and Jen continually worked on many of the strategies listed earlier to help him learn how to get started on his own. This wasn't a one-time conference where all was magically fixed. The beauty of the way we choose to confer now means that Jen could focus on ideas for a bit of time until Parker was eventually able to become more independent with it.

Now take a peek into Kristin's third-grade classroom. You will find that the strategies are pretty much the same; she can just push her students a little more into deeper thinking topics. Kristin often challenges her writers to dig a little deeper by thinking of times when they felt really strong emotions and listing ideas under those strong emotions. She also teaches them to use different graphic organizers when thinking through the major events of a story or the key ideas they want to

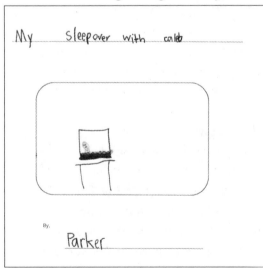

FIGURE 4.2
Parker's Sleepover Piece

teach in an informational piece. Kristin challenges her writers to create meaningful personal narratives by identifying times in their lives where they have felt really strong emotions. Like Jen, Kristin has several writers who are comfortable generating ideas and several who know that generating the idea is the hardest part of the writing process for them.

Chase is a kid who finds generating ideas to be a challenge, but once he has the idea, he can write independently. Kristin has learned that the only way to get her students to choose more meaningful topics is to model that same work. In the beginning of the year she often models lighthearted, funny stories for her writers but as the year progresses and the students mature, she models heavier topics. We can be vulnerable as writers and still keep our writing appropriate for our audience. When Kristin writes about giving away her first dog or when her little boy was rushed to the hospital, she is inviting her writers to choose more meaningful topics.

Georgia Heard spent some time in Kristin's classroom recently, and she taught the kids a new way of using heart maps to help writers choose more meaningful and more specific topics for nonfiction. Georgia taught Kristin's class that writers of nonfiction can begin generating ideas by thinking about why they are really interested in their topic. Writers can ask themselves what they love about their potential topic and jot those thoughts down on a heart map. After spending time thinking about why a writer is really invested in their nonfiction topic, they can build a second heart map where they jot down what they wonder. This will focus their topic and guide their research. Kristin noticed that Georgia's heart mapping really pushed writers to choose more meaningful and more specific topics.

If we can teach writers strategies for coming up with ideas, they will become more independent, confident, and better writers because they will produce more writing. That is why ideas is one of the six writing goals we teach to our students.

STRUCTURE

Structure calls for a writer's ability to present ideas clearly, with a logical, well-organized flow. Merriam-Webster's defines *structure* as "the way that something is built, arranged, or organized" (2016). Regie Routman says, "Present ideas clearly, with a logical, well-organized flow. Structure the writing in an easy-to-follow style and format using words, sentences, and paragraphs; put like information together; stay on topic; know when and what to add or delete; incorporate transitions" (2005, 13). "Great," you say. "Now what does this look like in a K through five classroom?" For us, it starts with kid-friendly definitions. We want to use language that is familiar and doable for kids. Otherwise the concept can feel out of reach. We teach our little ones that structure is like the bones of their writing that holds all their ideas together, or the building blocks that provide a strong foundation for their writing.

What Do the Common Core State Standards Say About Structure in Writing?

The Common Core State Standards for writing structure in kindergarten through fifth grade relate to opinion writing, informative/explanatory writing, and narrative writing. The standards increase in depth and complexity the higher the grade level. Here are the standards for kindergarten and for second grade set side by side to show how they progress:

Kindergarten	Second Grade
• Use a combination of drawing, dictating, and writing to compose opinion pieces in which they tell a reader the topic or the name of the book they are writing about and state an opinion or preference about the topic or book (e.g., *My favorite book is . . .*).	• Write opinion pieces in which they introduce the topic or book they are writing about, state an opinion, supply reasons that support the opinion, use linking words (e.g., *because, and, also*) to connect opinion and reasons, and provide a concluding statement or section.
• Use a combination of drawing, dictating, and writing to compose informative/explanatory texts in which they name what they are writing about and supply some information about the topic.	• Write informative/explanatory texts in which they introduce a topic, use facts and definitions to develop points, and provide a concluding statement or section.
• Use a combination of drawing, dictating, and writing to narrate a single event or several loosely linked events, tell about the events in the order in which they occurred, and provide a reaction to what happened. (NGA/CCSSO 2010)	• Write narratives in which they recount a well-elaborated event or short sequence of events, include details to describe actions, thoughts, and feelings, use temporal words to signal event order, and provide a sense of closure. (NGA/ CCSSO 2010)

For grade three, an additional standard related to writing structure says that students should

- With guidance and support from adults, produce writing in which the development and organization are appropriate to task and purpose. (NGA/CCSSO 2010)

For grades four and five, the standard says that students should

- Produce clear and coherent writing in which the development and organization are appropriate to task, purpose, and audience. (NGA/CCSSO 2010)

What Strategies Can You Teach to Strengthen Structure?

Although we've found that the strategies we teach for all six I SCORE qualities do follow a pattern, we do not move down the list checking off items one after another. Every student is different, and we pick and choose which strategies will help each child elaborate more successfully. Here are the structural elements we teach to kids so that they can use appropriate structure in their writing:

- Table of contents
- Beginning, middle, end
- Leads: question, noise word, suspense, action, dialogue, setting, time of day
- Endings: feeling, surprise, circular
- Paragraphing: a new person speaking, change of scene, passage of time, new topic
- Page design
- Glossary
- Bibliography

What Does Using Structure in Writing Successfully Look Like?

Canyon includes a strong lead after using *Crow Call* by Lois Lowry as a mentor text (Figure 4.3).

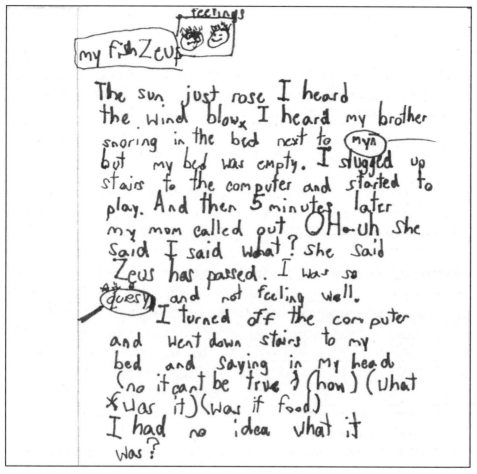

FIGURE 4.3
Canyon's Piece, "My Fish Zeus"

Spencer creates a five-paragraph essay making sure that he creates separate paragraphs for the introduction, three supports, and conclusion (Figure 4.4). Atticus creates new paragraphs when a different family member speaks.

- **What Should You Know Before Teaching Structure?**

Kids who love to build, like math, or just think logically tend to excel when they focus on structure. Bradley loves math but dreads writing. Kristin made it her

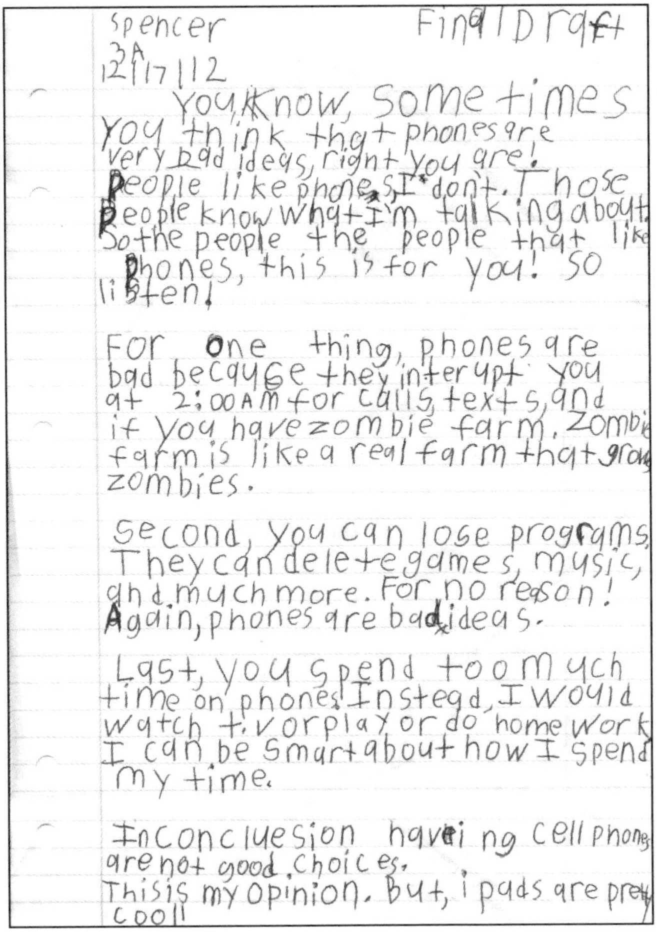

Spencer   Final Draft
3A
12/17/12
        You,know, some times
you think that phones are
very bad ideas, right? you are!
people like phones,I don't. Those
people know what I'm talking about.
So the people the people that like
  phones, this is for you! So
listen!

For one thing, phones are
bad because they interupt you
at 2:00AM for calls,texts,and
if you have zombie farm. Zombie
farm is like a real farm that grow
zombies.

Second, you can lose programs.
They can delete games, music,
and.much more. For no reason!
Again, phones are bad ideas.

Last, you spend too much
time on phones.Instead,I would
watch t.v or play or do homework.
I can be smart about how I spend
my time.

In concluesion have ing cell phone
are not good choices.
This is my opinion. but, i pads are prety
cool!

FIGURE 4.4
Spencer's Final Draft

mission to teach Bradley that writing did not have to feel as painful as when he started the year with her. Bradley was the Chihuahua kid. Kristin would teach a mini-lesson, send the kids off to write, and by the time she started her first small group or conference Bradley was tapping her on the shoulder. If she did not respond to the tapping quickly enough he began frantically jotting his concerns on sticky notes and sticking them next to her. His notes said things like HELP!!! and I MEAN IT!!! or CAN'T DO THIS!!! or IS IT TIME FOR MATH YET??? And yes, there were always three exclamation points. Bradley did not feel comfortable writing independently. Bradley often talked about his love of building with Legos and his love of math. Kristin decided to teach Bradley the building blocks of writing. They worked on strong leads, strong endings, paragraphs, transitional phrases, topic sentences, and multiple fonts. When Kristin began a unit on persuasive essays, she asked Bradley to let her know what he thought about writing at the end of the unit. Several weeks later Bradley raised his hand and said, "Mrs. Ackerman, you were right: writing isn't so bad after all!" Bradley loved the predictability of essays. He knew that he would write five paragraphs with an introduction, a conclusion, and three supporting paragraphs. Bradley had no problem using transitional phrases or creating new paragraphs. It was during the unit on essays that the finger tapping and the frantic sticky notes ended. Kristin was able to design specific strategies to help Bradley create structure in his writing. Now he is well into middle school and although he would still choose math over writing any day, he can confidently produce essays for his English class because he was taught the specific strategies to do so.

What Might Conferences Around Structure Look Like?

Jen sits with Haley, a first grader who is writing a book called *How to Take Care of a Cat*. "Hey, Haley, how is your writing going today? Can you read me some of what you are working on?" asks Jen. The title suggests that the book will be a how-to type of format but as Haley reads her work it seems to be more of a list of randomly put-together ideas and sentences. Jen's first thought is that if Haley had a way to structure her piece, her ideas could be grouped together in ways that made sense to the reader. "Haley, you have done such a nice job of sharing what you know about cats in this book. Thanks for teaching me that I should not give cats human food. I don't have a cat, so I wasn't sure about that." Haley smiles. Jen continues, "So, Haley, for someone like me who doesn't know a lot about cats, it sure would be great if you would think about how you could teach me what you know by putting all the same ideas together so I could go to a page and know just what it was about." Jen shows Haley how creating a table of contents before she starts writing would help her organize what she wanted to write on each page and help her reader by putting the same ideas together. "Haley, what sentences do you think might go together?" Jen asks.

Haley replies, "Well, this sentence about beds could go with the parts about food and water because cats need those things."

"Great thinking, Haley. What might you call that section?"

"Umm, maybe things cats need?" she replies. From there, Haley decides on her next draft to create a table of contents with the following headings: "What cats need," "Why people should have cats," and "Why I love my cat." She is able to take the sentences she has written already and group them in an organized way. We talked earlier about how these goals all end up intertwined. The bonus of this work is that Haley's focus automatically improves along with the structure because her sentences fit together under the heading.

If Haley had chosen not to revise this piece that would be fine with us as well. The hope is that on her next piece she will think about how a table of contents might be a first step to helping her as a writer and that is what this work is all about. Jen will keep checking in with Haley, reminding her how a table of contents might help her as a writer and looking for evidence of the strategy in her writing.

Now take a peek into Kristin's third-grade classroom.

"Mrs. Ackerman, I need you!" Mimi whines.

"No problem, Mimi. What's going on?" Kristin asks.

"I don't know how I want to end my story," Mimi says as she looks at Kristin with a scrunched-up forehead and a look of concern.

"Can I show you what some writers do when they are not sure how they want to end their writing?" Kristin asks.

"Okay," Mimi replies.

"When writers want to have a strong ending they can include how they feel at the end," Kristin says. "Let's look at *Fireflies* by Julie Brinckloe." Kristin has read this book to the class so Mimi is familiar with it. After rereading the last page Kristin says, "Mimi, do you notice how Julie writes that the main character is smiling as tears fall down his face?"

"Yes, so she is explaining that he is sad but he knows he did the right thing by letting the fireflies go . . . or maybe he is crying tears of joy," Mimi comments.

"So, let's look at your draft. How might you include what you are feeling?" Kristin asks.

"Hmm . . . Well, after my friends and I sailed through the rain, the ocean calmed down and I wasn't scared anymore. I waved to the ocean when we got back to shore and I felt calm and said goodbye. The ocean almost feels like a really strong, powerful person so I said goodbye and I wasn't scared of her anymore," Mimi talks out.

FIGURE 4.5
Mimi's piece, Sailing in Maine

"Sounds like you have a great way to end your sailing adventure!" Kristin replies (Figure 4.5).

Teaching kids strategies for creating structure in their pieces will not only help their writing make logical sense to their reader, but also help them create a plan for sustaining writing. When we were writing this book, the first thing we did was create a table of contents. We used it to help keep us focused and include all the information we wanted to share. Because structure is vital to good writing and crosses all genres, we make it one of our overarching goals for writing.

CONVENTIONS

Conventions are the systematized rules of language and writing. Children have to produce letters and words; employ editing and proofreading skills; and use accurate spelling, punctuation, capitalization, grammar, legibility, and formal rules of a genre. We teach our writers that conventions are the "rules of writing," the nitty-gritty of the writing that enable a reader to read what is written, but conventions should not be considered the only and all when it comes to writing instruction. In an article for Choice Literacy, Heather Rader describes conventions perfectly. She says, "*Yes,* I believe conventions need to be taught to all children to give them access to a literate life. *So,* conventions need a place in our writing instruction. *And,* conventions should not take precedence over the instruction on writing content, organization and style" (2016). They are the basic element that all writers must use; conforming to the rules of conventions is the only way a writer gets his point across. All else is lost if the reader cannot understand what a writer is attempting to communicate.

NCTE's beliefs about teaching writing include the following statement:

> Readers expect writing to conform to their expectations. For public texts written for a general audience, contemporary readers expect words to be spelled in a standardized way, for punctuation to be used in predictable ways, for usage and syntax to match that used in texts they already acknowledged as successful. They expect the style in a piece of writing to be appropriate to its genre and social situation. With that in mind, writers try to use these surface elements strategically, in order to present the identity, create the relationships, and express the ideas that suit their purpose. (NCTE 2016)

What Do the Common Core State Standards Say About Conventions?
The College and Career Readiness Anchor Standards for Language say that children in kindergarten through fifth grade should

- Demonstrate command of the conventions of standard English grammar and usage when writing or speaking.
- Demonstrate command of the conventions of standard English capitalization, punctuation, and spelling when writing. (NGA/CCSSO 2010)

The English Language Arts Standards for Language say that children in kindergarten through second grade should

- Use words and phrases acquired through conversations, reading and being read to, and responding to texts. (NGA/CCSSO 2010)

The English Language Arts Standards for Language call for children in second through fifth grade to

- Use knowledge of language and its conventions when writing, speaking, reading, or listening. (NGA/CCSSO 2010)

What Strategies Strengthen Conventions in Writing?
Here are some strategies we use to teach conventions. We strongly suggest that you look at the grammar and mechanics that your school or district require you to cover and adjust them accordingly.

- Stretching out words
- When in sight, spell it right
- Writing neatly
- Using spaces
- Using capital letters
    -at the beginning of a sentence
    -for names
    -for *I*

-for proper nouns

-for proper adjectives

-for common nouns when used as a name

-for the first word of a sentence inside quotation marks

- Punctuation

    -period

    -exclamation point

    -question mark

    -quotation marks

    -punctuation before ending quotation marks

    -commas in a series

    -commas after transitional phrases

    -commas with complex or compound sentences

- Proper use of conjunctions in a compound sentence
- Parts of speech

What Does Using Convention Skills Successfully in Writing Look Like?

Emilie is an avid reader and a typical perfectionist. Emilie pays attention to the conventions strategies that Kristin teaches and uses them pretty consistently (Figure 4.6).

Emilie is able to use basic conventions regardless of the genre she is writing in.

What Should You Know Before Teaching Conventions?

When it comes to conventions we need all hands on deck. Conventions have to be taught and reinforced all day long and in every subject. When students are writing an observation in science they can be reminded to write complete sentences. Shared reading is an easy time for a teacher to "think out loud" and notice conventions. "Hmm, I am noticing that the writer capitalized that word because it is a proper noun." When students answer a word problem in math, they should be expected to apply the conventions that they have been taught. The rules of writing should apply to all writing, not just writing workshop. Habits have to be practiced frequently before they become a natural, consistent part of our lives. If writers are expected to follow the rules of writing only during writing workshop, we are robbing them of the opportunity to build consistency.

"How come you get to sit in the front seat?" Daisy asked.

"Because I'm special. Duh," Maggie said.

"I've been here way longer than you," Daisy said. "I'm seven! (Well 49 in dog years) You're still a puppy."

Daisy said.

"I told you, I'm special. It's easy, like eating a dog treat. I'm the new dog. I get treated better," Maggie said.

"I, I, I. Me, me, me," she said.

"Daisy, Maggie! Time for bed," Stephon said cheerfully in his loud manly voice.

Daisy started sniffing frantically...

WAIT!" she said.

"What WHAT?" Maggie started to get excited even more every second.

FIGURE 4.6
Emilie's Piece

Lucia, a second-grade teacher, expects her second graders to write complete sentences on spelling tests. She takes points off if a student does not include periods. Kristin's son, Banyan, lost points on his spelling test and she e-mailed Lucia to thank her for holding him accountable. Lucia responded by saying that she often gets parent complaints through e-mail or in written notes on the spelling test. Fortunately for Lucia's students, she has been teaching long enough that the sad faces and negative notes from parents do not sway her. She cares enough about her students to allow them to have consequences when they do not use the skills that she is teaching. A spelling assessment is an appropriate document to expect correct spelling and complete sentences.

Now that we have established that conventions work happens all day, we can address how we manage to teach conventions during writing. When we work with writers we typically carry around mentor texts with us to use when teaching conventions. When we notice that a writer is not capitalizing proper nouns or not using dialogue, we can easily open up a familiar book to guide him or her. Every now and then we encounter a kid who feels like he has a compelling argument for why he needs ten ellipses and we gently remind him that we use mentor texts because our mentors are using the qualities of good writing and *selling* books. We have found that students are often more receptive to the work of published writers than to the voice of a classroom teacher. We know a teacher's voice can feel a little Charlie Brown (wah, wah, wah, wah-wah-wah-wah) so having a mentor text to look at can help break up the monotony. We look to authors just like an athlete looks to a coach.

What Might Conferences on Conventions Skills Look Like?

When Kristin first started teaching writing she often felt that the only things she could see in student writing were the missing capitals and periods. Although she was helping her writers to improve their conventions, she was not always able to celebrate their voice or their ability to elaborate. As Kristin learned more about writing, her conferences changed. Now Kristin compliments students on their ability to stay focused, their imagery, or their strong leads before diving into teaching conventions. As writers we are all more open to instruction after we have heard one way in which we are succeeding. So when we sit down with a writer and she reads her piece, we often say something like, "Wow, you have done a great job including the setting! I can totally picture where you are! I did notice that you are missing quotation marks when there is talking . . . Mind if I show you how to add those in?" Doesn't that sound a lot less threatening than "Well, I don't know what you are saying out loud because you don't have any dialogue . . ." We have made the mistake of leading with what is wrong, not because we are heartless, but because we didn't know how to look at a piece of writing and identify what was going well and what still needed attention. Now we often think of ourselves as general practitioners; when we look at student writing we have to ask questions, look at the writing carefully, and then begin triage—what needs the most attention? Sometimes conventions need to be the focus of a conference but they are not the only thing we confer about.

Hannah had been working on adding in quotation marks to show where people were talking in her piece. The next step was to make sure that she had beginning and ending punctuation inside the dialogue. Kristin was able to use a mentor text to show Hannah the proper way to punctuate. After Hannah revised with Kristin, Kristin asked her to finish on her own, using the piece of mentor text as a reminder if she needed it. It is easy to point out grammar errors to children and have them quickly correct the error, but they will not learn to use grammar properly if we continue to do it for them. Grammar is always a big part of the conversation when we go to workshops, read online articles, or meet with teachers. We use a gradual release of responsibility: we model, work with the writer, and then back out to allow him or her to attempt the work independently (Figure 4.7).

Kristin noticed that Sofia had a convention issue, but she suspected that the root of the problem was a lack of focus. Sofia actually shocked Kristin when they sat down to confer. Sofia said, "I really want to make sure that I am writing complete sentences." When they looked at her writing it was obvious that Sofia had gone back and reread her writing and made a few adjustments on her own. She was feeling really proud of her writing, but it was still littered with incomplete

FIGURE 4.7
Hannah Uses a Reference Book of Mentor Texts on Using Quotation Marks

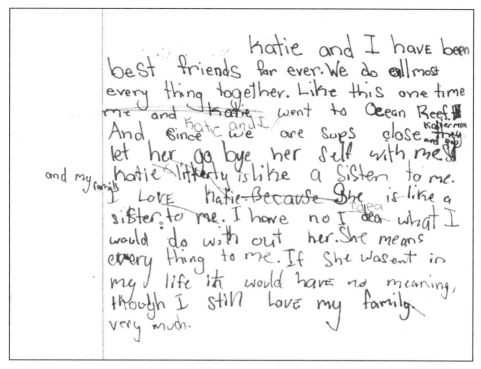

FIGURE 4.8
Sofia's Revised Draft

sentences. As Kristin looked at Sofia's writing she wondered if Sofia's problem was her inability to write a complete sentence or if Sofia was aimlessly writing about her feelings regarding her best friend, which created a lack of focus. Kristin decided to try first talking to Sofia about her focus and then looking at her sentence structure. We have talked a lot about having a relationship with our students; Kristin knows that Sofia can speak in phrases when she is really excited, but tends to speak in complete sentences when she is relaxed or calm. Knowing Sofia guided Kristin to try coaching Sofia's focus before tackling her conventions. The conventions needed attention, but without a focus she would be left with a piece that was adrift (Figure 4.8).

When Sofia drafted a second time, staying focused on the time she and Katie were swimming in the ocean and encountered fire coral, her sentences were a lot clearer. Kristin's next step was to teach Sofia how to use quotation marks to make the dialogue clear to the reader, but overall her sentences were a lot clearer.

This is probably the easiest of the six goals to teach. When we go into schools or do workshops with teachers and put up student writing pieces to discuss, the first thing teachers notice is conventions. They are easy to see, quick to fix, and within the comfort zone of how we were all taught to write. As teacher educators, we learned less from our professors about how to get kids to use voice and focus in writing and more about conventions through the red marks we got back on our college papers, so it is no wonder that this is where we tend to go first in conferences. We would like to be a bit scandalous here—because this goes against even our own school's beliefs, where the focus in writing is pushed largely toward conventions work—and say that this has become the last thing we work on with our own kids. We know that kids need to have writing conventions mastered so others can read their work. We encourage you to notice, and teach conventions to help your writers grow, but please, don't ignore the other great writing goals you could be teaching your kids and that will make their writing truly stand out.

A soccer player has to be a really good runner in order to play the game; players run several miles in each game. But if soccer players only ran and never scored a goal, the game would be pointless. We view conventions as an essential part of writing, just like running is to a soccer player. However, a writer's mastery of conventions without the ability to elaborate or write with voice is pointless. Writing encompasses more than one's ability to write a perfect sentence. Conventions are essential, but they should not be the only quality a teacher looks at to determine a writer's success.

ONE FOCUS

Kathleen Cali writes, "Focus is the feature of Effective Writing that answers the question 'So What?' An effective piece of writing establishes a single focus and sustains that focus throughout the piece." She goes on to say, "Focus, therefore, involves more than just knowing *what* your story is about, but understanding *why* you are writing it in the first place" (2013).

We teach our students that focus, simply put, is the one thing you are writing about, and we teach them strategies that help them develop that focus throughout the entire piece. This is a basic concept but is arguably the most essential part of a draft. If a writer cannot stay focused on one thing, the writing falls apart.

What Do the Common Core State Standards Say About Focus?

The Common Core State Standards are similar in grades K through five but increase with depth and complexity as appropriate for higher grade levels. The Common Core State Standards call for children in first grade to

- With guidance and support from adults, focus on a topic, respond to questions and suggestions from peers, and add details to strengthen writing as needed. (NGA/CCSSO 2010)

For grades three through five, the standards say that students should

- Write informative/explanatory texts to examine a topic and convey ideas and information clearly. Introduce a topic . . . and group related information. (NGA/CCSSO 2010)

What Strategies Can You Teach to Strengthen One Focus?

- Posting your main idea with a sticky note as you move from page to page
- Making sure each sentence relates to your main idea
- Identifying your audience
- Finding the heart of your story
- Deciding what really matters here
- Making sure everything fits
- Understanding broad topics versus focused topics

What Does Using One Focus in Writing Successfully Look Like?

A writer is writing with one focus when he writes about one thing. That one thing or topic might have other, more specific topics (like in a nonfiction book), but the writer holds on to one big idea and does not deviate.

Sofia writes with one focus in Figure 4.9.

FIGURE 4.9
Sofia's "No Christian" Piece

NO Christain !!

We were all exhausted but joyful and excited. We were all on about 4 airplanes and landed in Aspen, Colorado to come house to live in. "We're here," Mom said. "It's pretty cool," Christain said. "Let's check up-stairs," I said. "I agree," Dad said. When we got half up the stairs, We all saw a glass case covering a real bear that had died, or a

fake bear and it looked like it was near the month fall with leaves of yellow, gold, red, and orange. It was a beautiful sight. After a few minutes we kept climbing stairs there must be a hundred stairs, I think to myself. After That, we all decided what rooms that we'll pick to sleep in. Once we were done pick-ing what room would be ours, me and Christian asked if we could watch a movie. "Okay, do you want to watch Wallie?" Mom asked. "I'll set it up for you. Where do you want to

watch it?" Dad asked. "Let's watch it in Mom's room." I said to Christian. "Okay," Christain said When we got half up the stairs we admired the bear again. Not a word was said util we got up the stairs. When dad help-ed us put the movie on, we figured there were alot of commercials before we got to watch Wallie. Just when it start-ed Christian had to go to the bathroom. But before he did, dad asked mom to keep a eye on us because he had some work to

do. Just when mom got up the stairs, Christian called "Hey Mom look at this cool sink! And where's the soap? Mom rushed into the bath-room like a rocket. And I was running after her to keep up. Then she froze like a ice sculpture. After a few minutes, She said aloud, "Thats not a sink, thats a bidet!! (with means something that washes your butt sound out by-day) I laughed and laughed until everyone joined in.

What Should You Know Before Teaching One Focus?

Having one focus is an important strategy for young writers to learn early on. It not only teaches the kids to think about their audience and who they are writing for, but also gives their pieces purpose. They learn to understand why they are choosing to write about one specific topic and the importance of getting their point across in ways that make sense to their readers. No one wants to leave his readers thinking, "Huh?" When we were revising this book, we kept going back to our focus on our audience and what we wanted this book to truly be about. Learning to develop one focus is an essential skill for all writers.

Focus and elaboration tend to have an oppositional relationship. Children who are great at elaborating often tend to lose focus; children who are great at staying focused often struggle to elaborate. Brynn is a perfect example. She is a witty writer who can go on and on, but her ability to elaborate sometimes spins out of control when she writes personal narratives, essays, and journals. When Kristin meets with Brynn they often focus on making sure she ends her writing sooner. Kristin has taught Brynn that she has to plan before she can write and she has to stick to her plan. She gives Brynn a story arc when she writes narratives, comics, or fiction. She teaches her how to list a thesis statement when writing essays or a table of contents when writing nonfiction. As the school year progresses, Brynn is able to identify her own strengths and weaknesses as a writer and can use the strategies independently that Kristin taught her.

What Might Conferences on One Focus Look Like?

First grader Dasha loves to write. She rarely moves from her seat during writing time and her pencil never leaves the paper. Dasha's struggle is not that she can't get enough writing practice; she writes voraciously. She just tends to write and write with no clear plan of what she wants to write *about*. Jen sits down next to Dasha as she works on an information piece about dolphins. She has created a table of contents, so she knows *what* she wants to write about. As Jen reads through the writing, though, she realizes Dasha sometimes gets away from the focus or heading of the chapter.

Jen begins the conversation with, "Hey, Dasha, how is your writing going today?"

Dasha replies, "Great. I am writing about dolphins!" Dasha begins to read Jen some of the writing she has underneath the heading "Splash" (Figure 4.10).

"Dolphins make a big splash! When they jump up and down up and down. Dolphins are mammals too. Did you know that? Well, I will tell you."

So of course, the first thing Jen wants to point out is the great choice of voice Dasha uses in her piece. Information writing is much more interesting when the writer talks to readers and gets them involved in the piece.

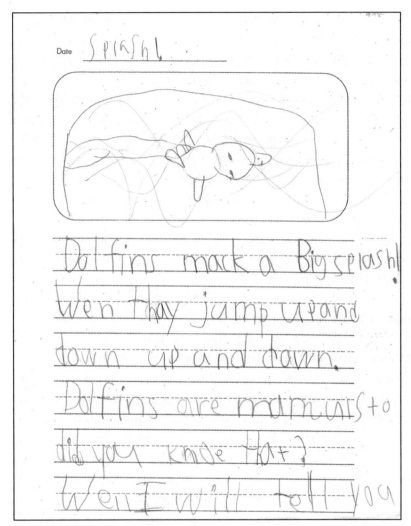

Date _Splash!_

Dolfins mack a Big splash!
wen thay jump up and
down up and dawn.
Dolfins are mamuls to
did you know that?
Well I will tell you

FIGURE 4.10
Dasha's Piece, "Splash"

"Dasha, when you wrote, 'Did you know that?' in your piece, it made me feel like you were teaching facts just to me. That is a great way to use voice in your writing," Jen compliments. She continues, "There was just one part that made me a little confused. Are you okay with me asking about it?" Dasha nods.

"Well, it looks like from the title that this is going to be about how dolphins splash, and you teach your reader that here. But then you start talking about how they are mammals and I got just a little bit confused. One thing you might want to think about as a writer is making sure that your chapter stays focused on one thing so your reader doesn't get confused. Can I show you a strategy for how I do that in my own writing?"

Sweet Dasha nods again.

"Okay. To keep my writing focused, I think about what I want to teach or tell, and then I make sure my sentences are all about that one thing."

Jen and Dasha read each sentence to see if they relate to the main idea of "Splash." When they get to "Dolfins are mamals," Dasha realizes right away that this doesn't really have anything to do with how dolphins splash in the water. As they talk, she realizes that she could write about how the fins and bellies smacking on the water as they dive back down might be what makes the splash and decides to write about that to keep her chapter focused. As Jen leaves Dasha, she reminds her that no matter what kind of writing she is doing, Dasha will want to make sure that as a writer, she remembers to keep her pieces focused by making sure her sentences match the heading of the chapter. For the next few conferences, Jen will be checking in to see if Dasha is able to do that independently or will need more support.

Sophie loves to write, and elaboration is not something that she struggles with. When left to write she can produce fourteen to twenty pages in a week. Sophie's writing starts off with focus, but she loses it as the page numbers increase. When Kristin confers with Sophie, they often have conversations about focus.

"Sophie, it has been a few days since we met and you already have several more pages written," Kristin comments.

"Yep!" Sophie answers.

"We have talked a lot about your ability to elaborate and we have also talked about not losing focus while you elaborate." Kristin follows up from a previous conference. "Sophie, what do you really want to teach your reader in this chapter?"

"I want the reader to learn about what turtles eat," Sophie says.

"Okay. Well, let's reread your chapter together and if we get to a sentence or a paragraph that is not teaching the reader about what turtles eat we can decide if we need to cut it or put the information in another chapter," Kristin coaches. Sophie and Kristin work on several pages, eliminating sentences here and there and bringing her piece back into focus.

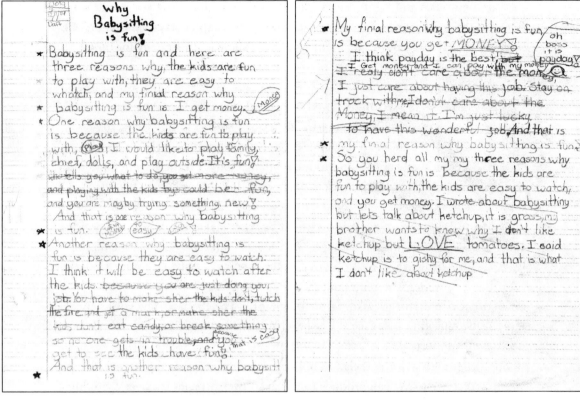

FIGURE 4.11
Elena's Piece, "Why Babysitting Is Fun!"

Elena was struggling to stay focused within her supporting paragraphs during an essay unit. Kristin gave her a sticky note for each support and Elena was given the task of reading each sentence and asking herself, "Does this fit my support?" As Elena went through the process she was then able to cut several sentences that did not support her essay topic (Figure 4.11)

As writers grow they begin to identify their own struggles. Zach was writing about a boating trip that he took with his family, but he was stuck. When he sat down with Kristin he told her that he couldn't continue writing until he figured out if he needed to include his dad's friends, who followed his family on another boat. He was quite bothered by the idea of excluding a group of people. Kristin asked him what his story was really about and he said it was special because of the time that he spent playing on a sandbar with Christian. After talking through his problem Zach decided that he could briefly mention that his dad's friends followed his family to the sandbar but he didn't need to say much more about them. Zach realized that his writing could lose focus if he spent too much time explaining who was at the sandbar that day.

Another important aspect of focus is to know your audience. Banyan, a second grader, and his little sister, Leila, love Christmas. They are in the habit of writing notes to their Elf on the Shelf named Red. Banyan does not love to write (even though his mom is writing this book!); however, when he has an audience that is important to him, he can spend hours writing. Banyan spent three hours one Saturday listing all the Pokémon cards he was hoping to get from Santa. His letters are focused because he knows his audience.

In the end, we want to make sure that our young writers know who they are writing for and the purpose of what they are writing—the why—so that their pieces can remain focused and on point.

REAL VOICE

Lisa Donohue describes voice in writing as follows: "Readers are able to gain an insight into the author's thoughts. We are able to hear the author reading, talking, sharing his or her words with us. The writing seems to come alive in our minds" (2011, 7). Ayres and Shubitz add, "We should let our students know that thinking about every mark they make on a page, as a writer, creates voice in their writing" (2010, 72).

We tell our kids that voice is simply writing in a way that sounds like how you talk. Sounding like yourself when you write. Knowing your audience and to whom you are writing. As Donohue says, "It is a way of connecting with an audience" (2011, 7).

What Do the Common Core State Standards Say?

The Common Core State Standards don't celebrate voice as much as we do since there is no specific focus on using voice to strengthen writing mentioned. We know, as teachers of writing, that voice is what sets writing apart. No matter what genre, voice is what makes a writing piece noticeable and unique. Voice is all about writers knowing who they are and using their own personality to charm, persuade, inform, or share with a reader.

What Strategies Can You Teach to Strengthen Voice?

Here are the strategies we use to teach voice:

- You, I (speaking directly to your audience)
- Asking "Who am I writing this for?" (knowing your audience)
- Asking the reader questions
- Using conventions creatively
- Storyteller or narrator?
- Using internal thought—*writing with italics*
- Using point of view
  - -first person
  - -second person
  - -third person

What Does Using Voice in Writing Successfully Look Like?

Last year Jen had Lizzie in her room. Lizzie wrote about meeting her best friend, Katie, for the first time. She started her piece, "Hi Katie. Hi Lizzie. Hey, do you want to go on the monkey bars? Well you go first, said Katie. Ok, I said but I fell down. Then Katie went and I thought, wow!" By using dialogue and writing in the first person, Lizzie was able to show all the feelings she felt meeting her friend for the first time. After describing more about the morning they met, she finished her piece with, "So do you know how fairy tales always end in happy endings? Well this one does. Katie turned out to be my best friend." The surprising fairy tale connection she made at the end helps the reader connect to Lizzie's humor as a writer and access the emotion she feels about her friend. The reader can't help but chuckle in awe at the ending of this piece. We feel like we really know Lizzie and her best friend, Katie.

Mimi has a unique writing voice; her word choice is so unique and powerful that her writing is almost poetic (Figure 4.12). When Kristin asked Mimi how she writes with such an unusual sentence structure she said, "Well, I think about what I want to say and then I move the words around a bit."

Kristin pushed her further and asked, "But you seem to choose your words so carefully. How do you go about choosing such powerful words?"

"Well, I was lying in bed thinking about what I would write and that was when I came up with *clear* and *smerky*, because the ocean looks clear but when you step in, the sand makes it all smerky." Mimi is thinking about images and then using those images to create sentences. Mimi's draft begins with this paragraph:

> *Clear, smerky, all I see as I enter the ocean blue. Swishing, swishing, the current pulls me back to the rock covered beach. The wind blows like a*

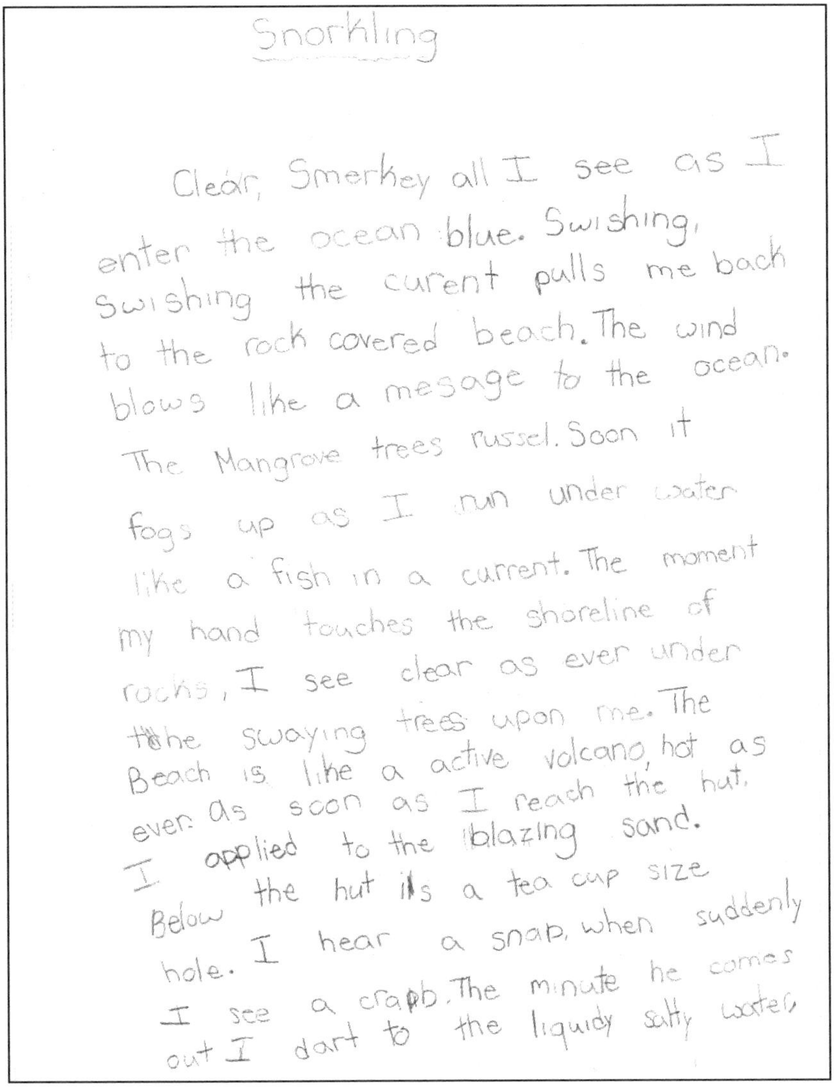
Snorkling

Clear, Smerkey all I see as I enter the ocean blue. Swishing, swishing the curent pulls me back to the rock covered beach. The wind blows like a mesage to the ocean. The Mangrove trees russel. Soon it fogs up as I run under water like a fish in a current. The moment my hand touches the shoreline of rocks, I see clear as ever under the swaying trees upon me. The Beach is like a active volcano, hot as ever. As soon as I reach the hut, I applied to the blazing sand. Below the hut its a tea cup size hole. I hear a snap, when suddenly I see a crab. The minute he comes out I dart to the liquidy salty water.

FIGURE 4.12
Mimi's Piece About Snorkeling

message to the ocean. The mangrove trees rustle. Soon it fogs up as I run under water like a fish in a current.

Mimi is a word collector in life without even realizing it. She is able to recall interesting words that match her images.

Krish transfers his love of making people laugh into his writing. He calls his sister a "mean-ager" instead of a teenager when he writes about her. He says she is mean only because she is a teenager and that eventually it will go away. Krish also likes to make a statement and then add an additional thought. He does this in every genre, from comics to nonfiction. In a comic about Mustache Man fighting an evil villain named the Bald Bandit, Krish writes about Mustache Man spraying the Bald Bandit with a weapon, the hair grower backer. One frame said this:

> *With all his might, Mustache Man takes his weapon, Hair Grower Backer. He hopes the villain will be good again. By the way, it's 30% off at your local hair spray store.*

Krish uses phrases like *by the way* to add voice. He wrote a sentence in his nonfiction book about killer whales. Krish wrote

> *Orca are the biggest type of dolphin. (And yes, its a dolphin)*

Krish used parentheses to add a note to the reader.

Robby talks to the reader and uses words that he uses in his everyday life:

> *Did you know that octopuses have three hearts? It is very crazy, I know and another epic fact about octopus body is that . . . some octopuses have venom.*

When Robby speaks he uses words like *epic*, so when he adds them to his writing, the reader can enjoy the flavor of his voice.

What Should You Know Before Teaching Voice?

Because voice is a complex skill to teach we tend to rely heavily on mentor texts. Marissa Moss and Michael Ian Black don't know it but they are teachers in

Kristin's classroom. Their books teach her kids what voice sounds like. Likewise, students who write with voice often share their writing as a model for what we are looking for.

As we said earlier, voice is all about writers knowing who they are and using their own personality to charm, persuade, inform, or share with a reader. One of the easiest ways to teach voice is to use mentor texts.

Knowing your audience is another great strategy for helping kids write with voice and helping readers use real voice in their work. Ruth Ayres and Stacey Shubitz remind us, "As a writer, I know my audience plays a large role in the choices I make. When I'm writing for children, I make different choices than when I'm writing for teachers. When students don't take into account their audience, their writing suffers" (2010, 266). At the end of the year, Jen asks her first graders to write a letter to their future second-grade teacher telling a bit about themselves. By knowing her audience, Hanna was able to add great voice to her writing and not only tell the teacher a bit about herself but, more important, show part of her humorous personality.

Voice is one of the trickiest of the qualities of good writing we teach to kids. Teaching strategies for developing a voice, of course, increases the chances that kids will be able to use voice in their writing, but we find over and over that some kids just have it intuitively. Jen's son, Will, has always written with voice. Whenever she picks up a piece of his writing, she knows it is his. He always writes directly to the reader and invites them in, through word choice, to join the journey he is about to embark on. Whether it be a narrative or expository piece, his sense of humor always shines through. Jen is fully confident that when it comes time for him to write his college essay, he will find a way to stand out from others through his use of voice. Many teachers, especially in the upper grades, may not appreciate reading voice in writing as much as we K–5 teachers do. Voice is usually one aspect of writing that can get tamped down as teachers demand writing that is formulaic. We argue that voice has a place in all writing if done correctly, respectfully, and well.

As writing teachers, we may find it hard to describe voice sometimes, but we know it when we see it. When we are reading voice in a writing piece, something might make us chuckle, or think, "Clever move, there," or surprise us.

What Might Conferences on Voice Look Like?

After reading *The Book with No Pictures* by B. J. Novak, Leila, a kindergartner, wants to try to write just like Novak. Kristin asks her, "What is it that you love about the book, Leila?"

"It is just so funny! It has naughty words and it makes me laugh even though there are not any pictures to look at!" Leila replies. She goes on to say, "I want to make you laugh with my own book!"

"What are some things that you could try to do that B. J. Novak did?" Kristin asks as they flip through the pages of the book.

"Stop," Leila commands. "This is it, this is the page I love because it makes you say such a naughty word and you *never* say naughty words!" She has stopped on the page that says, "My only friend in the whole wide world is a hippo named Boo Boo Butt" (Novak 2014, 27).

"I want to write about Boo Boo Butt. I want to tell his story!" Leila says while laughing.

"Leila, I think that you are liking this book because B. J. Novak writes with a lot of voice."

"He makes me think more about the words because there are not any pictures," Leila says.

"Would you like to try writing your story using naughty words and leaving out the pictures?" Kristin asks.

"Yes, I am going to write about Boo Boo Butt and just tap out my words," Leila responds. "Can I go now?"

"Yes, off you go. I can't wait to read it!" Kristin answers.

When Kristin sits down with Olivia, she sees that she is writing a piece about a Christmas trip. "Olivia, I am noticing that you have a lot of writing. Wow . . . three whole pages!" Kristin compliments.

"Yes, I loved this trip so it felt easy to write about," Olivia responds.

"Yesterday I taught a lesson about how writers include dialogue to help the reader understand what is going on in a story. I am noticing that you don't really tend to use a lot of dialogue" Kristin says.

Olivia stares back at Kristin with a hint of an eye roll and says, "I don't like using dialogue. I don't talk that much."

"Olivia, you make a good point. I have noticed that you seem to be more of an observer. Would you agree?" Kristin asks.

"Yes," Olivia replies.

"I would like to show you something that writers can do to communicate without using dialogue. Writers often use what I call internal thought. They share what they are thinking in their head," Kristin explains. "For example, when I wrote about my brother getting bitten by the dog, I added in a sentence that said,

> This does not look good, I think to myself. My stomach is full of butterflies and I think the old guy walking his dog is not paying attention.

"So, Liv, I did not say any of these things out loud; they were thoughts in my head that I included. Do you think you could try this out in your writing since you are not really a fan of dialogue?" Kristin asks.

"Let me look." Olivia pauses to read her writing. After a few moments she says, "Well, after we got on the plane for our trip I wondered how long the ride would take."

"Great, Olivia. Here is a sticky note. Write that down and then see if you can include what you are thinking at least one more time on your own," Kristin coaches.

Although developing voice is challenging to teach, we like to think of it as the value-added element of the qualities of good writing.

Hugh Gallagher won a Scolastic Art and Writing Award in 1990 with this satire on a college application essay:

> *3A. Essay: In order for the admissions staff of our college to get to know you, the applicant, better, we ask that you answer the following question:*
>
> *Are there any significant experiences you have had, or accomplishments you have realized, that have helped to define you as a person?*

> I am a dynamic figure, often seen scaling walls and crushing ice. I've been known to remodel train stations on my lunch breaks, making them more efficient in the area of heat retention. I translate ethnic slurs to Cuban refugees. I write award-winning operas. I manage time efficiently. Occasionally, I tread water for three days in a row.

I woo women with my sensuous godlike trombone playing, I can pilot bicycles up severe inclines with unflagging speed, and I cook Thirty-Minute Brownies in twenty minutes. I am an expert in stucco, a veteran in love, and an outlaw in Peru.

Using only a hoe and a large glass of water, I once single handedly defended a small village in the Amazon Basin from a horde of ferocious army ants. I play bluegrass cello, I was scouted by the Mets, I am the subject of numerous documentaries. When I'm bored, I build large suspension bridges in my yard. I enjoy urban hang gliding. On Wednesdays, after school, I repair electrical appliances for free of charge.

I am an abstract artist, a concrete analyst, and a ruthless bookie. Critics worldwide swoon over my original line of corduroy evening wear. I don't perspire. I am a private citizen, yet I receive fan mail. I have been caller number nine and have won the weekend passes. Last summer I toured New Jersey with a traveling centrifugal-force demonstration. I bat .400. My deft floral arrangements have earned me fame in international botany circles. Children trust me.

I can hurl tennis rackets at small moving objects with deadly accuracy. I once read *Paradise Lost, Moby Dick, and David Copperfield* in one day and still had time to refurbish an entire dining room that evening. I know the exact location of every food item in the supermarket. I have performed several covert operations with the CIA. I sleep once a week; when I do sleep, I sleep in a chair. While on vacation in Canada, I successfully negotiated with a group of terrorists who had seized a small bakery. The laws of physics do not apply to me.

I balance, I weave, I dodge, I frolic, and my bills are all paid. On weekends, to let off steam, I participate in full-contact origami. Years ago I discovered the meaning of life but forgot to write it down. I have made extraordinary four course meals using only a mouli and a toaster oven. I breed prizewinning clams. I have won bullfights in San Juan, cliff diving competitions in Sri Lanka, and spelling bees at the Kremlin. I have played Hamlet, I have performed open-heart surgery, and I have spoken with Elvis.

But I have not yet gone to college.

You can't read this essay without laughing! This writer connects with his audience, he makes us laugh, and he reminds us of that smart, witty friend we love to hang out with. Wouldn't he make it to the top of your yes pile?

We know voice is not the easiest of the six goals to teach, but when kids nail it, their writing is unique, funny, and the kind of writing we think college admissions people would love to read and are looking for in this next generation of kids.

ELABORATION

When we think about elaboration as a quality of writing we need to define what it is. Merriam-Webster defines elaboration as something "made or done with great care or with much detail . . . having many parts that are carefully arranged or planned" (2016). According to Regie Routman, to elaborate is to add appropriate details and facts to stated main ideas; explain key concepts; support judgments; or create descriptions that evoke mood, time, place, and the development of characters (2005).

The kid-friendly definition of elaboration we use with our students is "elaboration is helping your reader to see, hear, taste, feel, and understand what you are trying to write about."

We teach our writers that elaboration is all about helping your reader create a movie in their mind. Making facts and information memorable and relatable. Elaboration is *not* singularly focused on a writer's ability to write more; instead it's helping the reader create a mental image as the goal. Volume does not always equal quality; we do want our children to increase the volume of their writing, but not at the expense of meaningful work. Jeff Anderson writes in his book *10 Things Every Writer Needs to Know*, "Detail should be plentiful without being flowery or overdone. Powerful detail illuminates without overwhelming, explains without boring to death" (2011, 2).

What Do the Common Core State Standards Say About Elaboration?

There are a lot of standards that address elaboration. Writers are expected to draw, dictate, and write in an effort to compose narrative writing, informative/explanatory texts, and opinion writing. One really great thing about Common Core is that students are continually working on improving as writers and each year they are expected to demonstrate an increased ability to elaborate. The groundwork that is laid in kindergarten of drawing, dictating, and writing about a single event leads to a writer's ability to narrate a well-elaborated event and include detail to describe actions, thoughts, and feelings in higher grades.

In kindergarten writers are expected to

- Use a combination of drawing, dictating, and writing to narrate a single event or several loosely linked events, tell about the events in the order in which they occurred, and provide a reaction to what happened. (NGA/CCSSO 2010)

In second grade writers are expected to

- Write opinion pieces in which they introduce the topic or book they are writing about, state an opinion, supply reasons that support the opinion, use linking words (e.g., *because, and, also*) to connect opinion and reasons, and provide a concluding statement or section.
- Write informative/explanatory texts in which they introduce a topic, use facts and definitions to develop points, and provide a concluding statement or section.
- Write narratives in which they recount a well elaborated event or short sequence of events, include details to describe actions, thoughts, and feelings, use temporal words to signal event order, and provide a sense of closure. (NGA/CCSSO 2010)

What Strategies Can You Teach to Strengthen Elaboration in Writing?

Following is a list of strategies we teach that fall under the overarching goal of elaboration in writing. When we look at a child's writing and find that he uses a distinctive voice in his writing and that structure seems to be in place but that the writing lacks volume and/or details, we may decide with the child that elaboration is a goal he can be working toward as a writer. The elaboration strategies we have come up with are as follows:

- Labeling a picture

- Elaboration in illustrations: setting, character, action
- Using speech bubbles
- Show, don't tell
    - -writing interesting captions (compare, describe, explain)
    - -WOW words, not boring words! (WOW words give readers more specificity: *big* versus *humongous*.) Juicy words! (titles, chapters, anywhere!)
- Asking yourself, What else?
- Partner sentences
    - -compare
    - -give examples
    - -explain/define
- Zooming in—small moment
- Finding the heart of your story and writing more about that
- Embellishing
- Setting a mood/tone
    - -weather
    - -dialogue
- Be a movie star, not a narrator!
- What are you feeling?
- Creating internal and external character traits

What Does Using Elaboration Successfully in Writing Look Like?

We tend to find that the more our students read, the stronger their writing is. Cade is a great example. At nine he is reading the Lemony Snicket series, *The Hobbit* (with his dad), the I Survived series, and more. His writing reflects his reading (Figure 4.13).

A writer who includes action, dialogue, and setting in narrative writing is elaborating successfully. Writers of informational text attempt to persuade, teach, or inform by elaborating, or including relevant and detailed information.

What Should You Know Before Teaching Elaboration?

Elaboration is one of the most enjoyable of the six goals to teach. There are endless strategies and mentor text examples for enticing kids to tell their readers more. It is a strategy where we see the most growth in the shortest amount of time. Once

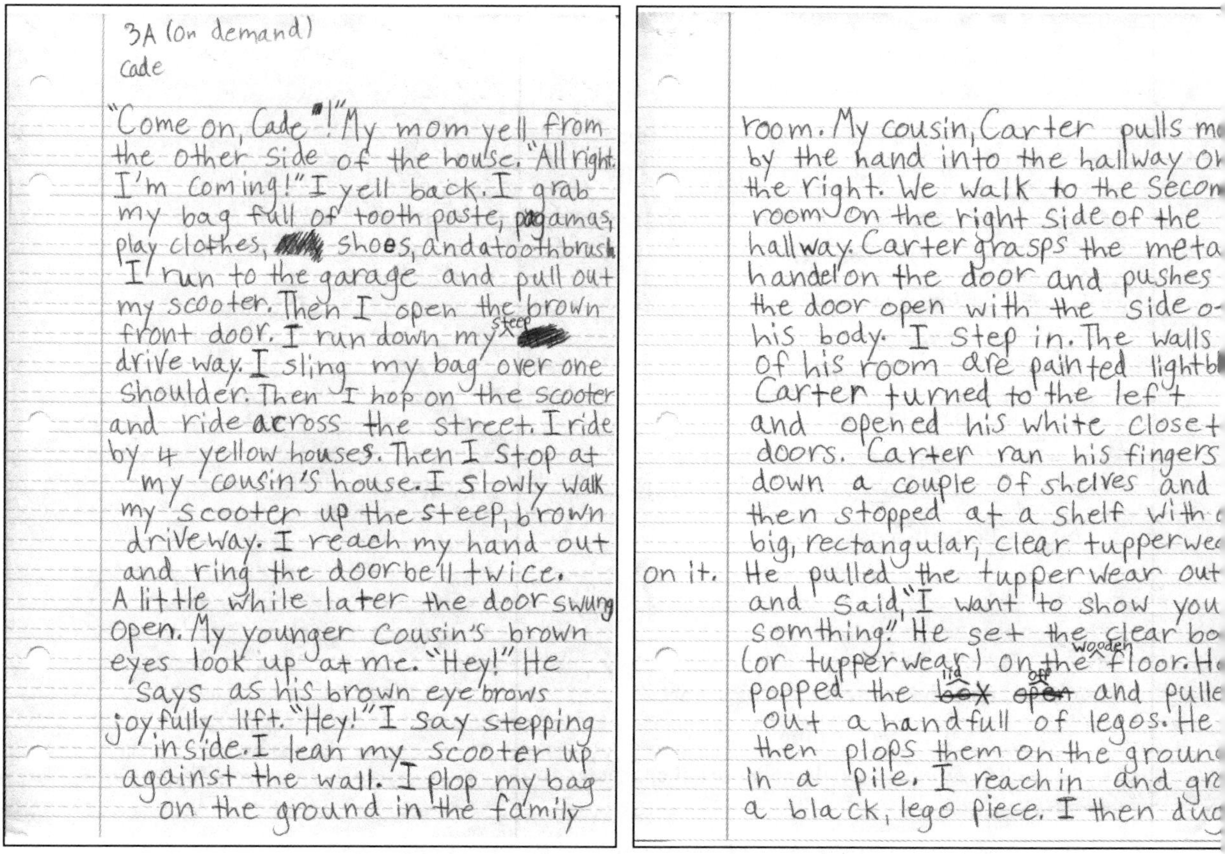

3A (on demand)
Cade

"Come on, Cade #!" My mom yell from the other side of the house. "All right. I'm coming!" I yell back. I grab my bag full of tooth paste, pajamas, play clothes, shoes, and a toothbrush I run to the garage and pull out my scooter. Then I open the brown front door. I run down my steep drive way. I sling my bag over one shoulder. Then I hop on the scooter and ride across the street. I ride by 4 yellow houses. Then I stop at my cousin's house. I slowly walk my scooter up the steep, brown driveway. I reach my hand out and ring the doorbell twice. A little while later the door swung open. My younger cousin's brown eyes look up at me. "Hey!" He says as his brown eye brows joyfully lift. "Hey!" I say stepping inside. I lean my scooter up against the wall. I plop my bag on the ground in the family

room. My cousin, Carter pulls me by the hand into the hallway on the right. We walk to the second room on the right side of the hallway. Carter grasps the metal handel on the door and pushes the door open with the side of his body. I step in. The walls of his room are painted lightb Carter turned to the left and opened his white closet doors. Carter ran his fingers down a couple of shelves and then stopped at a shelf with a big, rectangular, clear tupperwea on it. He pulled the tupperwear out and said, "I want to show you somthing!" He set the clear bo (or tupperwear) on the wooden floor. H popped the box open and pulle out a handfull of legos. He then plops them on the groun in a pile. I reach in and gr a black, lego piece. I then duc

FIGURE 4.13
Cade's Piece

students learn specific ways to elaborate, they can usually transfer the skill to their writing pieces pretty painlessly!

For the writer who struggles with elaboration, we ask ourselves questions such as the following:

"Is the writer still interested in his topic or does he need to consider choosing a different idea?"

"Has the writer lost focus?"

"Does the writer need a deadline?"

through the bin and pull out
4 black, small wheels. The I take
out a gray piece and another
black piece. After a while, I had
myself a black and gray lego car.
Then Carter and I heard, "Boys come
on out! Dinner's ready!" It was
my aunt. Carter and I dropped
our legos, shot up, and left the
room. Dinner was pizza. "Lets go
carter." I say finishing the last
bite of pizza crust. "O.k." Carter
says sliding out of his seat.
We walked through the hallway and
and opened a door on the left.
"Oh yeah. I forgot!" I say spinning
around. I run into the family
room and dig through my bag.
I pull out pagamas and a tooth
brush. I run into the bathroom,
slide on my pagamas, brush my te-
eth, & the next thing I know I'm
lying in bed in carter's room. It's dark.
It's silent, and I'm asleep. The End

If we can answer these questions, we can guide our writer toward a new topic, redirect the writer to gain focus, or provide a little pressure with a deadline.

What Might Conferences on Elaboration Strategies Look Like?

Figure 4.14 is a typical writing piece by a kindergarten author. As kindergartners and some early first graders begin moving their writing across pages, many have one sentence per page with strings of letters. You can see from the example piece that Whitney understands that nonfiction is about teaching. She draws detailed illustrations while writing a fact about her topic on each page. Because Whitney is

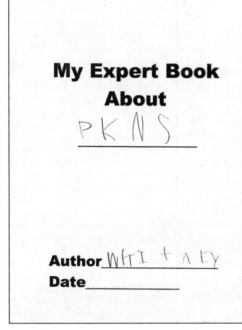

FIGURE 4.14
Whitney's Piece, "PKNS"

just learning to spell conventionally her writing can be hard to read. With a piece like this, Jen realizes that the next step for Whitney is to be able to convey all the information she knows about pumpkins without being held back by spelling. This provides a perfect opportunity to talk to Whitney about the elaboration strategy of labeling a picture to give the reader more information about her topic.

"Whitney, I can see as I read your piece that you know a lot about pumpkins. Not only did you put a lot of details in your pictures, but you also wrote a fact on each page. Your reader sure will learn a lot from you about pumpkins!"

Whitney nods her head enthusiastically and says, "I sure do know a lot about pumpkins. I get one every year from the pumpkin patch and bring it to my house."

Jen turns to the first page of the writing piece and points to the great details and fact on the page. "Whitney, tell me about this page. What do you want your reader to know?"

Whitney tells Jen, "First you need to give pumpkins lots of water."

NAMAJRS

NTNATATNE
BSS

TPNdTFRKSS

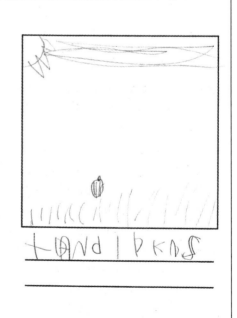

TANdIbKNS

"Oh," Jen says. "I see these drops coming down in your picture to give the pumpkin water. "Is that right?"

"Yep, lots of water from the rain!" Whitney says proudly as she traces the raindrops in the illustration with her finger.

"Oh, I see. That is rain coming from the sky. You know, Whitney, you are such an expert about pumpkins maybe you could help me out. Why do the pumpkins need the water falling from the sky like that?"

With a typical kindergartner "silly you" eye roll, Whitney says, "To help the pumpkins grow big."

"Ooh, now I get it. The rain helps the pumpkin grow big." Jen restates Whitney's thinking so she can hear it out loud. "So, Whitney, you taught me something new that wasn't even on the page. If I hadn't talked to you, I would not have learned such great stuff about pumpkins. You know, Whitney, because your reader won't always have you with them to explain all that extra good stuff, you may want to think about putting it in your book. One way you can do that is by labeling what is in your picture so the reader will learn even more from you."

Whitney's thinking but not yet committed.

"Like right here." Jen points to the drops. "You could put the word *rain* right by the drops in your picture and the reader would know right away that pumpkins need rain. Go ahead and try that out."

Whitney, who is comfortable with putting letters on a page to represent words, as you can see from her example, jumps right in and adds the word *rain* (rn) next to one of the raindrops.

"Whitney, do see anything else in the picture you might label to tell your reader more?" Jen asks to see if any of this is sinking in.

"Hmm . . . what?!?" Whitney replies.

Jen nudges on, "Remember when you said that the rain helps the pumpkins grow? What could you label in your picture to teach that?"

Whitney speaks up, "Oh, I know, by the pumpkin I could put *grow*" (she writes *g* and an *o* to represent the word *grow* since she is really focusing on beginning and ending sounds right now).

"So great for your reader, Whitney, to learn even more from you. Just know that you can always label the pictures in your writing to tell the reader even more. This helps the reader so much since you won't always be there to tell them what you know. You can write it down so it will always be there." Jen then nudges her a bit. "Do you think you could find some things to label on the next page to tell your reader more?"

Jen hangs out with Whitney for a minute or so more to see if she is getting the hang of the strategy on her own and makes sure to have Whitney share that day what she is trying out as a writer. If Whitney should choose not to go back and add things to her picture—and chances are she may not when Jen is not nearby—maybe she will put this strategy in her tool belt of elaboration strategies and use it in her next piece. Sticking close for a minute or two also gives Jen time to write down what she and Whitney have talked about that day. We have found that many kindergarten and first-grade kids do not go back on their own to revise. Once they're done with a piece, they tend to be done. But some do. Whitney might, and we want to be sure she has a strategy for getting better at elaborating in her writing. If a child does not immediately revise for the strategy in his piece, have faith that you have given the child something to think about in his next draft.

Please remember that this is only one of many strategies Jen could have chosen to teach Whitney based on her writing piece. They could have talked about tapping out words to get more letter representation, or thought about elaborating on the illustrations by drawing more. In this case, because Jen knows that Whitney usually has a lot to say orally about her writing, she decides to focus on elaboration as her overall goal and teach Whitney strategies for getting more of her thinking down on the page. Labeling the picture is just one way to help Whitney elaborate in her writing. Remember, like all the strategies we mention in this book, this strategy could be taught to the whole class or in a small group, depending on the need. Jen will talk further with Whitney about the idea of elaboration and what it is. She will also discuss this strategy again with Whitney and show her what she has written down. Sticking with one quality of writing for a bit of time will help Whitney be more focused in conferences. Instead of teaching Whitney something different every time they meet, Jen and Whitney can discuss what they talked about in the last conference and focus on a few more ways that writers elaborate, giving Whitney some time to get comfortable with using strategies all focused on the one big goal of elaborating in her writing.

Jen also meets with Erin, a beginning first-grade writer who is learning how to elaborate by adding partner sentences. When Jen meets with Erin she talks to her about how great it is that she is able to finish a whole book by herself, because writing doesn't come easily to Erin, and this is the first book she has completed

on her own. They then talk about how important elaboration is as a writing goal and about how the reader always wants to know more. Jen models in her own writing piece how to give each sentence a partner and say one more thing. They look at the first page of Erin's book and Jen prompts her with, "Why do you love Matthew?" Erin tells her and Jen suggests she could write that as her partner sentence. Jen leaves her with, "Erin, when writers write they want to tell the reader as much as they can. Today you not only told your reader that you love Matthew, but you told him why. Making sure each sentence has a partner is a great way to tell your reader more. Maybe you will think about that as you write more." When Jen goes back to check on Erin later, she finds that Erin has used the strategy to add partner sentences in the rest of her book independently. This is a great start! Jen will continue to focus on partner sentences with Erin until she can see that

Erin is using the strategy independently, and then she will move on to another strategy to help Erin elaborate in her writing (Figures 4.15 and 4.16).

Another elaboration strategy we use with kids comes from Georgia Heard's book *The Revision Toolbox: Teaching Techniques That Work* (2014). In this book, Georgia talks about how kids tend to give more details in their writing when they are taught to slow down time. In this minute-by-minute strategy, we ask our writers to write one short, simple sentence about their morning. For example, Will, a first grader, wrote, "I watched TV" (Figure 4.17).

When we asked him to slow the morning down into what he did minute by minute, you can see he included many more details about what he heard, saw, and smelled. This is exactly what we are trying to get kids to do when we ask them to elaborate more in their writing. After trying this activity with the kids (whole

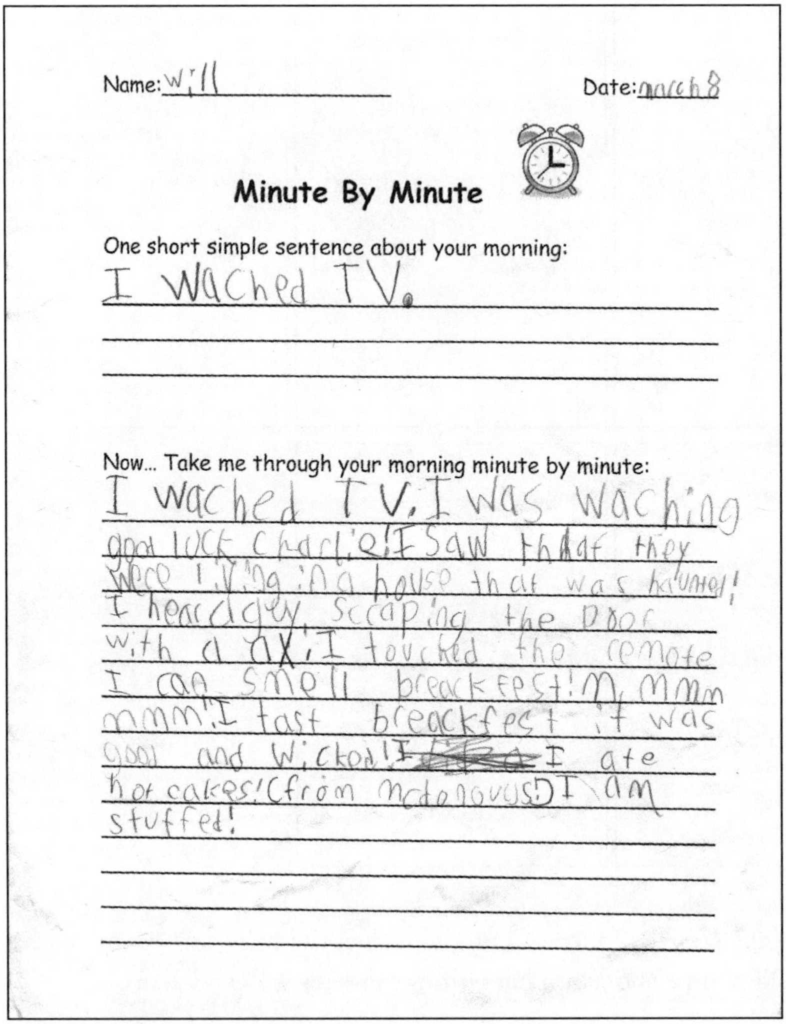

Name: Will   Date: march 8

Minute By Minute

One short simple sentence about your morning:

I wached TV.

Now... Take me through your morning minute by minute:

I wached TV. I was waching good luck charlie! I saw that they were living in a house that was haunted! I heard guy scraping the Door with a ax. I touched the remote I can smell breackfest! M, mmm mmm! I tast breackfest, it was good and wicked! I ate hot cakes! (from mcdonovus!) I am stuffed!

FIGURE 4.17
Will's Minute by Minute

groups, small groups, or individuals), we use the experience to remind them of how to do this in their writing on a day-to-day basis.

Now let's walk down the hall to Kristin's third-grade classroom. What strategies for elaboration might you see being taught there?

When Kristin sits down to meet with Maks, he is drumming his pencil on his desk, looking bored to tears. She asks him how it's going and he says, "I'm done!"

The first sentence of Maks's piece starts with "On a Sunday" . . . After only a few sentences, he runs out of steam.

"Maks, I notice that you seem to really enjoy writing about Gian, Ben, and Matt. They must be good friends of yours."

"Well, yeah, because we do a lot of crazy things and Gian and I are neighbors so we play together a lot," Maks replies. Maks, an only child, continues to talk about what he did on his playdate and how much fun he had. Kristin knows how much he enjoys playing with his friends because he does not have any siblings at home. Building a relationship with the writer helps Kristin to value what Maks values.

"Maks, I can see how excited you are about this story. Your whole face lit up as you talked about it," Kristin says. Maks smiles. "I noticed that you are telling me a lot more about your playdate than you wrote. What happened?"

"I don't know . . ." Maks gives a typical response.

"I think I know why you are having trouble so I am going to teach you something that could help!"

"Okay," Maks answers.

"I noticed that your writing is kind of summarizing your story. You are a bit like a narrator and so the reader is reading *about* your playdate, not reading as if it is happening right this moment. So your reader is missing out on all the really interesting parts of the playdate that you just told me about," Kristin explains.

"Huh, I think I get what you are saying . . . but what can I do?" Maks asks.

"One thing you can do is start your writing with action or dialogue. Let's look at my piece really quickly." Kristin reads the first few sentences of her writing.

The old swing squeaks as I pump my legs back and forth and back and forth. I look up and notice the late afternoon sun stretches out its lazy rays.

"What is different about my first sentence and yours?" Kristin asks Maks.

"Well, something is happening: you are swinging," Maks replies.

"Yes! I started with action. If you were to think about the first thing you did or said when you got to Ben's house, what would it be?" Kristin asks.

"Well, the first thing that happened is Gian and I walked into Matt and Ben's house," Maks answers after taking a few seconds to think.

"So, here is a piece of paper; why don't you write that down," Kristin says.

While Maks starts writing Kristin stays close by, but she takes a minute to jot down Maks's name to check back in with him the next day. She jots down group names for a new strategy titled "be a movie star, not a narrator!" and adds a good mentor text that she will use—*Crow Call* by Lois Lowry. Taking a minute to plan gives Maks space to write, but Kristin is still in close proximity so that he can check in if he needs help. She then walks around the room to peek over shoulders and add other students to her strategy group. At the end of writing workshop, Maks shares what he worked on with the class.

"Writers, what Maks shared today is a strategy that helps writers elaborate and I noticed several students who could share this goal with Maks and me, so we will check in with each other tomorrow."

As writers work on elaboration, it is not uncommon for them to begin to use run-on sentences. When writers have a goal of elaboration they are pushing themselves to write as much as they can. This often leads the writer to a new goal—conventions. We can celebrate their ability to elaborate and move on to the gritty work of conventions. We often find run-on sentences that sound something like ". . . and then . . . and then . . ." When we see this we teach our writers how to break their sentences into smaller chunks. Let's look at Cameron's writing (Figure 4.18).

"Hey, Cameron, I wanted to check in with you about the goal that you are working on," Kristin says to Cameron.

"Okay," he replies.

"So if we look at your draft, I can see that you are using a lot of strategies to elaborate! You started your piece with dialogue and you continued to use dialogue throughout your story. You also included the setting in your writing so that the writer knows where you are!" Cameron's smile continues to grow as Kristin points out several different skills that they have been working on. "Cameron, you even wrote over two pages! Do you remember when you first started writing in my room?" she asks.

"Yes, I couldn't write a full page," he answers.

"So I think you are ready to move on to a new goal. What do you think?" Kristin asks.

FOCUS: KEEPING SPECIFIC GOALS IN MIND

"Yes!" he replies with confidence. (If Cameron had said no, they could have talked about it and continued to work on elaboration. We have to listen to our students, and if we are asking questions we have to follow through with providing choice. Kristin knew she could continue to teach Cameron additional ways to elaborate so she was not stuck but she felt that it was important to move on to conventions.)

"Cameron, a lot of writers can start to write really long sentences when they are focusing on elaborating. The only problem is that our reader can get a little lost or confused if our sentences are too long. Let's look at your piece. Will you read it out loud?" As Cameron reads he laughs a bit sheepishly at the end of the first page.

"I wasn't really thinking about periods when I was writing. I was thinking about the story," he admits.

"Cameron, when I write I don't think about periods either. I often have to reread my writing several times and make adjustments! This might be an even bigger challenge for you because you speak, read, and write in Spanish, English, and Farsi. You have three languages swirling around in your brain."

"I know. Sometimes I realize that I am thinking in Spanish but writing in English," Cameron says.

"So this could be a good goal to work on, don't you think?" Kristin asks.

"Yes," he answers.

"The first thing I want to teach you is a strategy that you need a partner for. I will be your partner today and eventually you can use your writing partner for this strategy. I want you to read the first page of your draft again. Each time you pause to take a breath, I will tap your shoulder. Then you can check to see if you have a period. If so, great; if not, you can add one in and capitalize the next word to start the next sentence" (Figure 4.18).

As Kristin and Cameron continue to work on this strategy she can meet with Cameron and his partner and eventually challenge Cameron to tap his own shoulder or snap his fingers as he begins to notice that he is pausing. The goal is for Cameron to eventually read his own writing, identify run-on sentences, and revise them, but this takes time.

Grayson walks up to Kristin and asks for a meeting. Grayson says she can't write anymore and as she reads her piece out loud she stops and looks at Kristin and says, "I am the narrator, right?" Grayson realizes that she is summarizing and that is the reason her piece fizzled out. Kristin asks Grayson if she can begin again

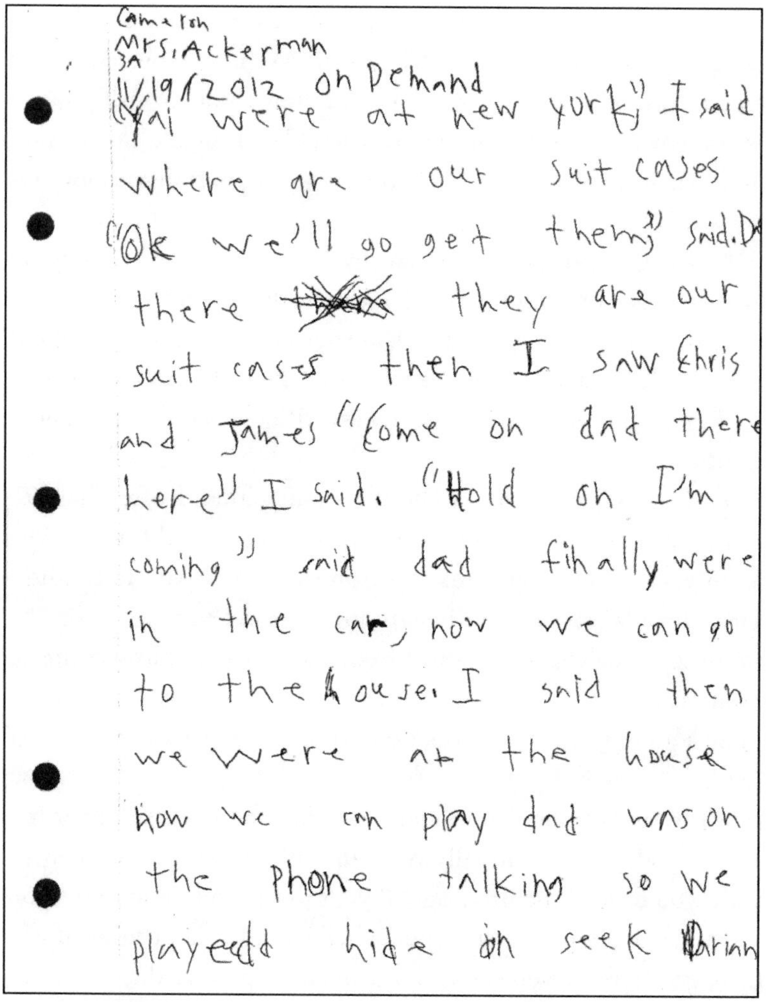
Cameron
Mrs. Ackerman
3A
11/19/2012 On Demand
"Yai were at new york" I said
where are our suit cases
"Ok we'll go get them" said. D
there ~~thers~~ they are our
suit cases then I saw Chris
and James "Come on dad there
here" I said. "Hold on I'm
coming" said dad finally were
in the car, now we can go
to the house. I said then
we were at the house
now we can play dad was on
the phone talking so we
playedd hide in seek Darian

FIGURE 4.18
Cameron's Piece, "New York"

with action. Her original draft begins with an observation and that makes it easy to narrate. Grayson adjusts her lead and she is able to tell her story moment by moment.

We have found that most kids elaborate in their oral language but can lose detail when overwhelmed by putting pen to paper. By teaching specific elaboration strategies, providing examples in mentor texts, holding kids accountable for elaborating, and celebrating when it is done well, most writing can and will improve.

⁂   ⁂   ⁂

The time we spend with writers one-on-one is critical. We have to be able to get in and out of a conference quickly and move on to other students, which means we have to be able to listen, assess, and make a quick decision about what we will teach a writer, teach our chosen strategy quickly and effectively, and move on. Conferring is one of the hardest things we do as teachers, yet when it is done well, it makes a huge difference in the lives of our writers. One of the benefits of using the qualities of good writing as a guide is that when we sit down with writers we have a map, and we know that we are going to choose a direction to head in by selecting one of six bigger goals to work on. This gives us consistency, so our conferring is less scattered. Both teacher and student have more clarity.

Please know that sometimes we sit down with a writer and are not able to make a quick decision. We are not afraid to look at a writer and say something like, "I want to do a little thinking before I meet with you," or "Can I take some time to think? I will come back to you in a few minutes." Sometimes our writers do something that we don't expect or we notice a lot that needs to be worked on and we are not sure what we want to coach first. Frankly, sometimes we need a little more than a few seconds to make a plan. Although this is rare, we are not afraid to take some time to think instead of making a mess of our opportunity to confer simply because we feel pressured to have something intelligent to say. This happened to Kristin the other day when Atticus showed her a chapter in his nonfiction book. Atticus titled the chapter "Scale Wise." The chapter was full of interesting sentences about numbers and how they related to a narwhal. The tricky part was that none of the sentences seemed to fit together and in the first reading Kristin was having a little trouble un-muddying the water and finding a way to guide Atticus into grouping his sentences into paragraphs. So after Atticus read the chapter Kristin said, "Atticus, you have such an interesting title. Can you tell me what you were thinking when you decided to write a chapter called 'Scale Wise'?"

"Well, I really wanted to talk about all the different numbers that I read about when I was researching narwhals," Atticus replied.

"That is really unique. I haven't worked with many writers who have grouped their information in this way," Kristin said. Atticus smiled and Kristin continued. "Atticus, you are teaching your reader in such an interesting way. If you don't mind I would like to do some thinking about this chapter before we meet again. I am thinking that we could work on creating paragraphs so that we chunk your sentences together in a way that will make sense to the reader, but your sentences all share different facts so I need a little more time. Can you work on another chapter for now and I will get back to you after P.E.?" Kristin was lucky because the class was heading to P.E. in fifteen minutes so she could take a little more time to look at Atticus's draft again before meeting with him. The sentences were all so different that she needed more time to come up with a solution.

Atticus happens to be a world traveler, an old soul, and a complete gentleman, so he responded, "Sure, we can do that." After dropping the class off at P.E., Kristin looked at Atticus's writing again and noticed that Atticus could group his sentences by creating a paragraph that included all the sentences about the physical numbers of the narwhal, how long they are, how much they weigh, and so on, and another paragraph on the information about how they live in pods.

One benefit to teaching students that there are several big goals to work toward and that those goals remain the same regardless of the genre is that we see a transfer from unit to unit. When we first started this journey, one of our primary questions was *Why don't we see a transfer of skills from genre to genre?* We knew that if we were both struggling with the same question, we were not effectively teaching our writers that the strategies we teach need to be used in all writing. Creating a plan for how we could intentionally and explicitly show our writers a few basic qualities that all writers need has given us a clear direction and helped our students to incorporate the strategies we teach and carry them over from one genre to another.

In May, Kristin sat down to confer with Robby. She noticed that his nonfiction writing was filled with voice. Kristin had been teaching lessons about text features and paragraphing, but she had not covered voice yet in the current unit. As she continued to meet with other writers she noticed that their writing was full of voice as well. Writers were talking to the reader, adding in Did you know? bubbles, and sharing internal thoughts in parentheses after an interesting fact. Her writers had been working on voice all year and they continued to use it in their final unit even though Kristin hadn't recently taught mini-lessons on it. Kristin was quick to stop the class and share what she had noticed, cheering her writers on, and then she continued to work with writers one-on-one. As the year progresses, the work should slowly get easier for the teacher and the students because we repeatedly focus on the same goals. When a person lifts weights frequently, he or she should grow stronger and the work should begin to feel easier. The same is true for writers.

When they know that they need to use all of the qualities of good writing they should be able to do so with greater ease as time goes by. Sometimes we are able to cut mini-lessons that we had planned because our writers have continued to use the skills that we have taught. When the majority of our class is using a strategy proficiently we move on and offer support to anyone who needs it one-on-one.

So, what happens when we notice that things are not going so well? Anytime that we find ourselves saying something like, "She can do it when I am sitting right next to her, but when she works independently she is not successful," we know that we are not releasing responsibility effectively. Interestingly, when we work with other teachers and look at our own practice, we notice a lot simply by paying attention to the body language of teacher and student during a conference. At the end of one writing unit Kristin asked other teachers to join her class in an effort to meet with all writers individually to make final revisions before they completed a final draft. Writers are usually looking for help with basic grammar and structure mistakes at this stage. Kristin pulled in coworkers who had a different schedule, student teachers, coaches, anyone she could! She returned the favor by going into her colleagues' rooms to help with editing conferences as well. As Kristin looked around the room she noticed that one teacher was sitting next to a writer and the writer was holding his draft and following along as the teacher read the draft out loud. The writer simply listened to his writing from the reader's perspective and stopped to add in a word or capitalize the beginning of a sentence as he listened. The writer was in control, and he was making changes. If he missed something, the teacher simply paused and asked, "Does that look right? Does it sound right?" The teacher nudged the writer to notice that something was off but did not swoop in and say, "Put a period here."

For another teacher working with a writer, the body language was very different. The teacher was holding the student's writing and had a pen in her hand to edit, while the child was staring out the window. The teacher had taken all the responsibility from the writer, and the writer was checked out. This is something that most of us have done. The teacher had every intention of helping the writer but ended up doing the work for the writer. The writer would be able to make the corrections that the teacher provided, but the writer would be dependent on the teacher. We don't expect a coach to lift weights for us at the gym, we don't expect a colleague to interview for a new job for us, and nobody is offering to pay our taxes for us. As teachers, we often get it wrong. We think we are helping when we are really holding our students back. For years, Kristin had to physically sit on her hands when she first sat down to confer with a writer one-on-one. It can be helpful to pay attention to how you approach a writer. If you notice that you are writing on the writer's draft, if you are unable to make eye contact with the writer because you are so busy "fixing" the writing, or if the writer is disengaged, you might be working too hard. That is not to say that we never touch a writer's draft, but we prefer to write a note or a suggestion on a sticky and hand it to the writer; we model a strategy in our own writing; or we look at a mentor text with a writer. We even point out something that a writer can do, watch him or her try it once or twice, and then give him or her the job of using the strategy moving forward. We hold the writer responsible for revising his or her writing.

In the end, we have been thrilled that our focus eventually led to a change in conferences. Instead of sitting down with a writer and identifying what skills need more coaching, the students begin to approach the teacher knowing which skills they want to work on. Kristin noticed this change in early spring when several students began approaching her with a problem and wanting to talk through how they were going to solve it. Zach was concerned that if he mentioned too many people in his small moment he would lose focus, Grayson realized that she was the narrator and she needed to be the movie star, and Sofia wanted to make sure that she was writing complete sentences. Because we are teaching the same skills all year our students are able to identify what is working well and what they want help with. The qualities of good writing do not change; they are consistent, and when we teach consistent skills frequently, our writers have a clear picture of what they are trying to accomplish.

We have also seen a change in student independence. Will, a third grader, sat down with a draft of his nonfiction book and decided to revise in the same way that Kristin had conferred with him all year. Will grabbed a stack of sticky notes and started making notes for himself of the revision work he wanted to do. He noted things like "change the font size," "add in a caption to explain where narwhals live" (after looking at a map that he had included), "capitalize the letter *t* in Table of Contents." Will was able to do this work because he had seen his teacher model it all year long.

Although we address the qualities of good writing one at a time throughout this chapter, the reality is that each quality is essential and a writer cannot be successful without the effective use of all the qualities simultaneously. A writer's ability to come up with ideas, stay focused, and elaborate all weave together. Ideas, focus, and elaboration constantly rely on each other in order for the writer to create something of quality. If a writer is struggling to elaborate, it is most likely because they did not choose a meaningful idea or they are unable to stay focused. Likewise if a writer is really good at elaborating he might struggle to stay focused. Conventions and structure are basic skills that all writers must use to create a piece that is readable, and voice allows the writing to stand out—it is what resonates with the reader.

By keeping these six important, overarching goals in mind as we work with kids, our conferences have become more focused, predictable, and routine for the kids. We are seeing more transfer of our teaching and feeling more prepared to talk to kids about their writing. We hope that by using this format, you too will find yourself more confident and ready to confer with your own writers!

CHAPTER 5

FOLLOW-UP: MAKING OUR TEACHING STICK

N ow that you have increased the frequency with which you meet with your students and have focused the work you do with them, it is time to make sure the kids actually use the strategies you are diligently teaching them. The third thread is follow-up. The things we do to follow up and make sure that our teaching is sticking may be the most important of all three threads. If we, as teachers, just *hope* our teaching points are clear but do not check in to see if kids are using the strategies we are spending precious classroom minutes on, then what is the point, really?

The ways that we follow up with children include

Assessment,

Pulling strategy groups,

Utilizing reference books,

Author shares, and

Celebrations.

This chapter highlights many ways we can go back to a child and say, "So, we talked about trying this in your writing. How's it going?"

ASSESSMENT

Assessment is the most important piece of follow-up. It is an essential tool to confirm what students can do independently after spending a period of time trying out specific strategies with support. In our classrooms we use two different types of assessment, formative and summative. These two types of assessments are used for very different instructional purposes and there is a place—a need—for both in the classroom. Formative assessments, as defined by Landrigan and Mulligan, "are frequent, ongoing, and incorporated into classroom practice so teachers can find the gaps between what students have learned and where they are struggling. They inform both teachers and students about student understanding at a point when timely adjustments can be made" (2013, 23). Landrigan and Mulligan then go on to say that summative assessment is, "The assessment *of* learning versus the assessment *for* learning. A summative assessment typically happens after a specific point in instruction to measure understanding of new learning or to evaluate the effectiveness of instructional programs" (2013, 23). In our classrooms, we use both kinds of assessment as a way to follow up with our students.

The formative assessments we use include pretests, note taking, student checklists, and reflections. We use formative assessment to plan conferences, strategies to be taught or reviewed, and possible next steps for instruction.

We begin each genre study with a preassessment. We ask each child to write for us in that genre before any formal instruction of strategies is presented. We give the class forty-five minutes and tell them to show us what they know. It is important for students to know that a pretest is really for the teacher to better inform the teaching, not for a grade. We use the drafts to help us see what strategies the majority of the class is already using so we can adjust what our teaching points will be in the weeks ahead. We use the preassessments to not only get a sense of what our writers already know about a genre, but also to assess for proper convention usage and carryover of strategies taught from the last genre study. Remember, one of the biggest concerns we had was how to get kids to use the writing strategies taught not only in the piece in front of them but in all their writing, no matter what genre. Looking at the preassessment drafts is another way to see if that kind of carryover is successful in our classrooms. We also use the preassessments to measure growth over time. The hope is always that the preassessment and the final draft of the genre will show not only growth and understanding of what was taught in other genres (conventions work, voice, structure, etc.), but also a command of the specific strategies used within that type of writing, such as strong text support if writing a literary essay or reliable research when writing an expository piece.

One of the ways that we ensure follow-up with our writers is through our note taking.

We have used many different forms for taking notes, as mentioned in an earlier chapter, because we know that documenting the work we do with our students is extremely important and guides our future instruction. It helps us to be accountable for following up with our writers. The documentation is critical, but *how* you document must be determined by personal preference and any school or district expectations. This formative assessment is what keeps the teaching momentum driving forward. We agree with Landrigan and Mulligan, knowing that "What is most important about taking conferring notes is that they help us remember the teaching priorities for each student. Once we ask questions and watch a student in the process of learning, we analyze what we have observed and decide on instructional goals" (2013, 77). This truly is how our note taking guides our one-on-one instruction. We teach a strategy, like adding partner sentences to build toward a bigger goal of elaboration, and continually watch for the strategy's being used in a student's writing. If we set this goal with a student and we see no evidence of partner sentences in the writing, we know we go back and reteach. If we see partner sentences being used appropriately and consistently, then we know it is time to move on to another strategy within that bigger goal of elaboration. We record our teaching moves and next steps so that the next time we meet with the writer, we can assess progress and either remediate or teach something new. We learned from Boushey and Moser in *The CAFE Book* (2009) that by using "Touch Points" to assess a student's progress we can easily see when a skill is mastered or not being used at all, and because our school uses a 0–4 system of grading skill development on report cards, the information can easily be turned into a grade. Our school grades are as follows:

0	not evident
1	below expectations
2	approaching expectations
3	meeting expectations
4	exceeding expectations

FIGURE 5.1
Kristin Is Using the CCPensieve to Confer with Atticus.

We use this language to help us decide where a child falls with the strategy as evidenced in the writing drafts. Each time we meet with a student, we record the grade. At report card time, we look at our notes and average the grade based on the numbers. Our notes are a constant form of assessment to drive our instruction and to think about bigger goals as well as to use as a grading tool.

Kristin has fallen in love with Joan and Gail's online CCPensieve (Figure 5.1). It is an easy, affordable comprehensive tool that keeps her organized. The CCPensieve allows you to create groups based on strategy need, to keep track of children you have met with, and offers countless other tools that will amaze and delight you! She has also found that typing in notes as she confers with a child is actually faster than handwriting them, which has actually decreased the time spent with each student. Jen is not quite as computer savvy as Kristin yet and has not fully committed to keeping all notes on the computer (Figure 5.2). Jen likes the way she can keep her notes and writing examples for each child together in a folder so that everything is in one place. She rotates the folders through the week to make sure that she has conferred with each child. She uses an adaption of the note-taking forms found in the back of *The CAFE Book* by Boushey and Moser. If you like having student writing accessible for conferences but feel like it is too overwhelming to travel with a computer and folder of student work, Evernote is another online tool to consider. This app not only lets you take notes on a student but also take pictures of student work, so previous work is at hand and ready to reference. You can also record conferences to use for grading or reminding the student of what was taught. You can check that out at evernote.com or look for Evernote in the Apple Store.

Maybe what we describe seems like too much to you. We often hear teachers say that they feel like they lose time supporting writers if they document everything

Writing Conferences With:		
Goal:		
Strategies: 1. 2.	**Strengths:** 1. 2.	
DATE	**OBSERVATIONS AND INSTRUCTION**	**NEXT STEPS TO MEET GOAL**
Touch Point	Writing Piece: Level: Notice: Teach:	Writer's Job: When do we meet next?
Touch Point	Writing Piece: Level: Notice: Teach:	Writer's Job: When do we meet next?
Touch Point	Writing Piece: Level: Notice: Teach:	Writer's Job: When do we meet next?
Touch Point	Writing Piece: Level: Notice: Teach:	Writer's Job: When do we meet next?
Touch Point	Writing Piece: Level: Notice: Teach:	Writer's Job: When do we meet next?
OVERALL OBSERVATIONS:		

FIGURE 5.2
Jen's Conferring Sheet Based on Boushey and Moser's Work from *The CAFE Book*

that they do with each kid, that taking the time to write things down keeps them from moving efficiently from child to child. We still believe that the notes you use to document student learning will help you clarify and drive next steps. If you are taking notes that aren't clear or focused, we can see why it would feel like a waste of time. These were the kind of notes we used to take before focusing on the qualities of good writing as our overarching goals. Our notes were random snippets like, "Used periods today—yay!" Then for the same student the next set of notes might say, "Great lead but needs to elaborate" and the next note might say something like, "Used a table of contents to organize piece but is forgetting capitals for names." This kind of unfocused instruction, the randomness of the notes, and the lack of a clear instructional path might leave you wondering what the point is. But once you have thought about ways that your conferences will be more focused around overarching goals, we believe you will see how helpful your notes will become to you. If you are still not sold, there is another option for quick in-and-out note taking: checklists (Figure 5.3).

	Structure	Table of Contents	Introduction	Bibliography	Paragraphing	Topic Sentences	Glossary	Multiple Fonts
Brynn								
Zach								
Taylor								
Krish								
Chase								
Cade								
Sofia								
Robby								
Meriel								
Logan								
Natalie								
Madison								

0	not evident	3	meeting expectations
1	below expectations	4	exceeding expectations
2	approaching expectations		

FIGURE 5.3
Structure Checklist

Checklists are another alternative to more comprehensive note taking, provide a helpful way to document what you are noticing, and take only a moment to fill out. As the classroom teacher, only you can decide what works best for you. Figures 5.4 and 5.5 show a few charts we use when planning writing units and the checklists that can be used within that unit to confer with.

Name: _____

Nonfiction Writing Checklist:

STRUCTURE

_____ Topic sentences for each chapter

_____ Uses multiple fonts (bold, different color, or different style)

_____ Creates new paragraphs when writing a new topic or idea

_____ Includes a table of contents

_____ Includes a glossary

_____ Includes a bibliography

CONVENTIONS

Capitalization

_____ Beginning of a sentence

_____ Proper nouns

_____ Title

_____ Chapters or headings

Ending Punctuation

_____ End of a sentence

Commas

_____ Commas in a series

Complete Sentences

_____ Writes clear and complete sentences

Word Choice/Spelling

_____ Applies appropriate spelling of word wall words

_____ Applies word patterns that have been taught

FOCUS

_____ Stays focused on one topic

_____ Has at least four separate chapters that teach about different information on that one topic

_____ Writes factual information

VOICE

_____ Talks to the reader with a teaching voice

_____ Uses "Did you know" bubbles to teach the reader

ELABORATION

_____ Uses comparisons

_____ Uses captions to explain pictures

_____ Uses pictures, drawings, diagrams, charts, or maps to teach the reader

---

FIGURE 5.4
Student Nonfiction Writing Checklist

We use student checklists with writers when they are finished drafting. This allows the writer to have a concrete list of strategies that he is expected to use within the unit before the work is assessed by a teacher. In younger grades we use picture cues; with older writers we simply list the strategies that were taught.

Reflections are also a great tool to inform instruction and set goals. Several times throughout the year it is helpful to pull out previous writing and allow students to look at what they have done and compare it to their current work. Writers can reflect on what their strengths are and then set goals for how they would like to

---

Name: _____   Date: _____

Personal Narrative Student Checklist

Structure

_____ Used action, dialogue, and setting to create a strong lead

_____ Wrote an ending that includes your feelings

_____ Story has a clear beginning, middle, and end

_____ Wrote 1–2 pages

_____ Created paragraphs (every time a different character speaks, passage of time, setting changes)

Capitalization

_____ Beginning of a sentence

_____ Proper nouns

_____ Letter *I*

_____ First word of a sentence in dialogue

Ending Punctuation

_____ End of a sentence

_____ Ending punctuation inside of dialogue

_____ Wrote complete sentences

_____ Wrote contractions appropriately

Examples
    did not: didn't
    I am: I'm
    is not: isn't
    does not: doesn't

_____ Spelled words correctly

_____ Stayed focused on your small moment

_____ Included internal thought

_____ Wrote a story and not a summary (Make sure you are the movie star!)

_____ Described the setting

_____ Wrote cursive neatly

_____ Included facial expressions

FIGURE 5.5
Student Personal Narrative Checklist

improve. These reflections are great for teachers to use so that when we confer we can help our students to work toward accomplishing their goals. It can be hard to allow students to guide our instruction, but when we do we are validating their thinking and empowering them to take their writing seriously. If you look at Carter's reflection (Figure 5.6) and his checklist (Figure 5.7), you can see that he is accurately identifying his strengths and weaknesses.

Mimi is also making accurate comments about her writing and Kristin follows up by writing back to her (Figure 5.8).

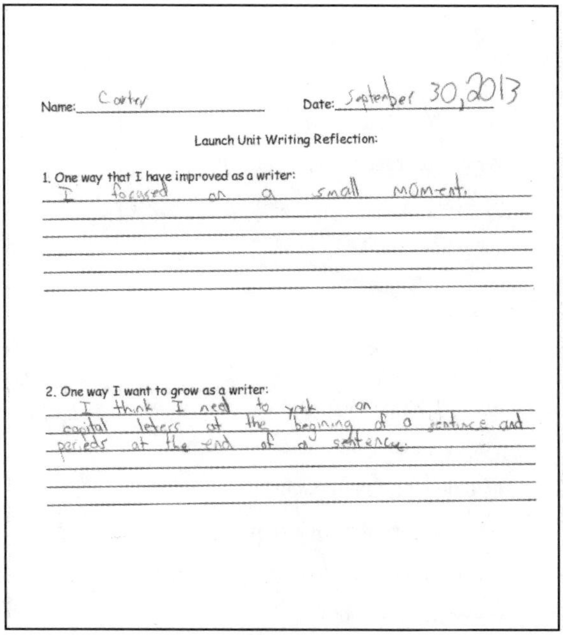
Name: Carter Date: September 30, 2013

Launch Unit Writing Reflection:

1. One way that I have improved as a writer:
I focused on a small mom-ent.

2. One way I want to grow as a writer:
I think I ned to work on capital leters at the begining of a sentince and pereds at the end of a sentence.

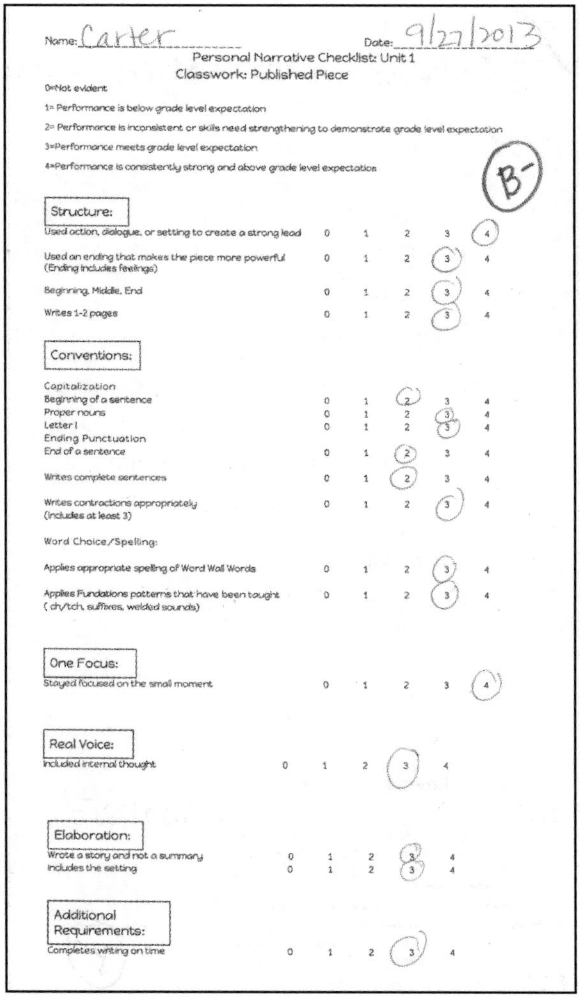
Name: Carter Date: 9/27/2013

Personal Narrative Checklist: Unit 1
Classwork: Published Piece

0=Not evident
1= Performance is below grade level expectation
2= Performance is inconsistent or skills need strengthening to demonstrate grade level expectation
3=Performance meets grade level expectation
4=Performance is consistently strong and above grade level expectation

B-

Structure:					
Used action, dialogue, or setting to create a strong lead	0	1	2	3	(4)
Used an ending that makes the piece more powerful (Ending includes feelings)	0	1	2	(3)	4
Beginning, Middle, End	0	1	2	(3)	4
Writes 1-2 pages	0	1	2	(3)	4
Conventions:					
Capitalization					
Beginning of a sentence	0	1	(2)	3	4
Proper nouns	0	1	2	(3)	4
Letter I	0	1	2	(3)	4
Ending Punctuation					
End of a sentence	0	1	(2)	3	4
Writes complete sentences	0	1	(2)	3	4
Writes contractions appropriately (includes at least 3)	0	1	2	(3)	4
Word Choice/Spelling:					
Applies appropriate spelling of Word Wall Words	0	1	2	(3)	4
Applies Fundations patterns that have been taught (ch/tch, suffixes, welded sounds)	0	1	2	(3)	4
One Focus:					
Stayed focused on the small moment	0	1	2	3	(4)
Real Voice:					
Included internal thought	0	1	2	(3)	4
Elaboration:					
Wrote a story and not a summary	0	1	2	(3)	4
Includes the setting	0	1	2	(3)	4
Additional Requirements:					
Completes writing on time	0	1	2	(3)	4

FIGURE 5.6 (ABOVE)
Carter's Reflection

FIGURE 5.7 (RIGHT)
Carter's Checklist

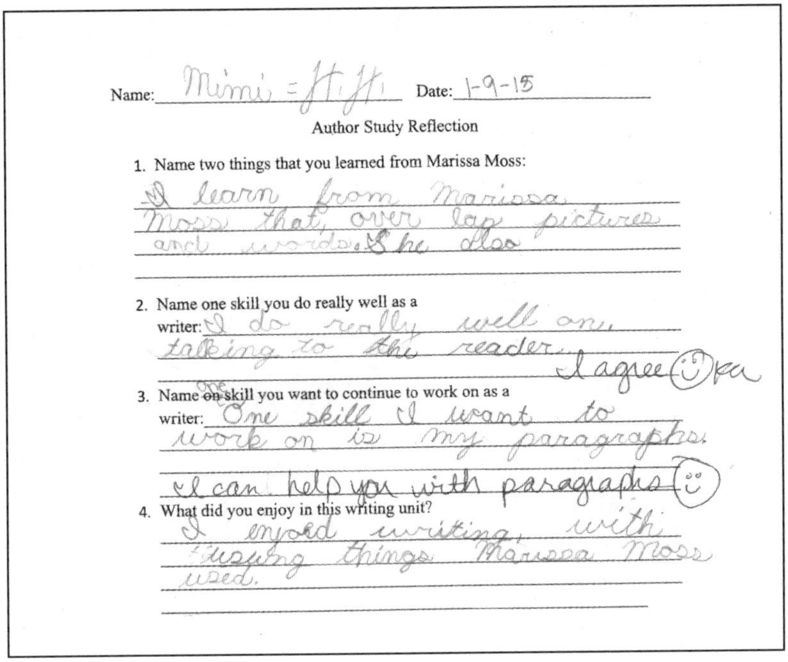

FIGURE 5.8
Mimi's Reflection

In the end, the formative assessments you and your students employ are only as good as the way you use them. Your assessments, notes, checklists, and reflections will be what you use for planning instructional time, conferring, and grading.

Our summative assessments take place at the end of a month or unit. We need formal assessments like this not just to determine next teaching moves but because we are all responsible for coming up with ways to grade for report cards and/or the developmental checklists that parents receive multiple times a year.

As mentioned, we give students a kid-friendly checklist of what they will be expected to do at the end of the unit. We expect writers to independently use the strategies that we have taught them and then we use the checklist to grade their writing. These assessments guide our future instruction and are used as a tool to determine where a student falls according to a grade-level standard.

At the end of a unit or genre study (which usually lasts about four weeks) we give a postassessment. This time we give our students a checklist so they know exactly what we are looking for and we tell them they have forty-five minutes to create a piece of writing.

Sophia did not feel like she had enough time to finish, so she wrote Kristin a note. The vast majority of our writers are able to complete an assessment within the time limits, but some of our writers who are really good at elaborating struggle to finish. The good news is that we are assessing all the qualities of good writing, so if a student fails to finish they still earn points for all the strategies they used. They lose points only in the structure section.

Writing can be a very challenging subject to grade, and it can be subjective. In an effort to assess with transparency we use a checklist that includes all the strategies taught over the course of a writing unit so students earn points for the different strategies that they implemented. We use our school's grading scale to compute a writing grade based on evidence of strategies implemented.

It is important to note that our checklists are usually the same for the writing that students create in class and for the assessment; however, for certain genres the assessment checklist is sometimes adjusted. For example, when we teach a unit that requires a lot of research, we do not expect our writers to research and then write in a limited time frame. Instead we provide information and ask our writers to write one page of a book instead of creating an entire nonfiction book within one writing block. We then remove some items from checklist, such as a table of contents. Because students are producing only one page, certain skills like a table of contents do not apply.

Our younger writers have shorter checklists and our older writers have longer checklists because our teaching builds on the work of previous years (Figures 5.9 and 5.10). We continue to hold third, fourth, and fifth graders responsible for simple convention rules like capitals and periods. A kindergartner might capitalize the beginning of a sentence but a fourth grader is expected to not only capitalize the beginning of a sentence but to also capitalize the first word inside of dialogue, proper nouns, headings, titles, and much more. Although the checklists might appear to look overwhelming in the older grades, they are really only building on familiar skills. As the year progresses, our writers are comfortable with longer checklists because we add only a few new skills each unit.

Name: _Dasha_____   Date: _12-9-13_

Nonfiction Checklist
On Demand Piece

0=Not evident

1= Performance is below grade level expectation

2= Performance is inconsistent or skills need strengthening to demonstrate grade level expectation

3=Performance meets grade level expectation

4=Performance is consistently strong and above grade level expectations

Parent
Signature

Structure:	0	1	2	3	4
Table of Contents	0	1	2	(3)	4
Writes 4-5 pages	0	1	2	(3)	4
Sentences in a logical order	0	1	2	(3)	4
Interesting Lead-uses a strategy taught	0	1	2	(3)	4

Conventions:					
Capitalization:					
Beginning of a sentence	0	1	(2)	3	4
Word I	0	1	2	(3)	4 N/A
Ending Punctuation:					
End of a sentence	0	1	(2)	3	4
Word Choice/Spelling:					
Correctly spells trick words taught they	0	1	(2)	3	4
Applied Fundations patterns that have been taught (consonants, short vowel, digraphs, bonus letters: f,l,s glued sounds, baseword suffix s)	0	1	2	(3)	4
Writes each sound heard- Taps out words	0	1	2	(3)	4
Correct letter formation	0	1	2	(3)	4

Focus:					
Section topic matches heading	0	1	(2)	3	4

Voice:					
Word choice reflects the reader's personality	0	1	2	3	(4)

Elaboration:					
3-4 Sentences per page	0	1	2	(3)	4

Additional Requirements:					
Stamina during Writing Workshop	0	1	2	(3)	4
Independence during Writing Workshop	0	1	2	(3)	4
Neat work	0	1	2	(3)	4

FIGURE 5.9
First-Grade Example

Name: Chase   Date: 5/18/2015

Nonfiction Writing Published Piece Checklist:

0	not evident
1	below expectations
2	approaching expectations
3	meeting expectations
4	exceeding expectations

Structure:

Title page	0	1	2	(3)	4
Table of contents	0	1	2	3	(4)
Included topic sentences for each chapter	0	1	2	(3)	4
Writes at least 4 chapters	0	1	2	(3)	4
Used multiple fonts (bold, different color, or different style)	0	1	2	3	(4)
Created a glossary	(0)	1	2	3	4
Included bibliography	0	1	2	(3)	4

Conventions:

Capitalize the beginning of a sentence	0	1	2	3	(4)
Capitalize proper nouns	0	1	2	3	(4)
Capitalize headings and titles	0	1	2	3	(4)
Includes punctuation at the end of a sentence	0	1	2	3	(4)
Writes complete sentences	0	1	2	(3)	4
Applies accurate spelling of word wall words	0	1	2	3	(4)

Applies word patterns that have been taught	0	1	2	3	(4)

One Focus:

Stayed focused on one topic	0	1	2	3	(4)
Each chapter focuses on one topic	0	1	2	(3)	4
Writes factual information	0	1	2	3	(4)

Real Voice:

Talks to the reader with a teaching voice	0	1	2	3	(4)
Used did you know bubbles to teach the reader	0	1	2	3	(4)

Elaboration:

Used comparisons	0	1	2	3	(4)
Used captions to explain pictures	0	1	2	3	(4)
Used pictures, drawings, diagrams, charts or maps to teach the reader (text features)	0	1	2	3	(4)

Additional Requirements:

Completes writing on time	0	1	2	(3)	4
Writes neatly	0	1	2	3	(4)

Grade: (A-)

FIGURE 5.10
Third-Grade Example

STRATEGY GROUPS

Another way we follow through with our writers is to pull together a strategy group (Figure 5.11). If you find yourself teaching the same strategy over and over in one-on-one conferences, then putting together a small group may save some time. Before planning small groups it is essential to walk around the room and identify what writers are doing when they write independently. It is important to schedule days where you don't confer with kids but research what writers are doing. Typically, we confer with writers four days a week and we research one day a week. The time taken to research allows teachers to effectively meet the needs of their students. Typically, we use an I SCORE strategy group planning sheet as we walk around the room. As we look over the kids' shoulders, we can get a sense of what is working and what still needs work and can jot down names of kids who need help with a specific skill. We have also talked a lot about how easy it is to notice convention errors. Strategy groups are a perfect way to handle those glaring issues.

We teach our small groups with the same structure that we teach whole-group lessons. We begin with discovery. Children are given mentor texts and we can ask them why they think a writer would do X and then we name the skill and look for more examples. Then we model the skill in our own writing. Finally, we have the kids look at their drafts and revise using the skill that we identified.

As we research we can also adjust our whole-group lessons; if the majority of the class needs help with a skill, it makes sense to teach it in a whole-group setting instead of pulling multiple small groups.

To hold the students and ourselves accountable, we make sure to note the small-group work on each student's conferring sheet with a Touch Point number from 0 to 4, just like we would in a one-on-one conference.

FIGURE 5.11
Jen Confers with Students in a Strategy Group.

REFERENCE BOOKS

Kristin came bursting in to Jen's first-grade classroom one afternoon, all abuzz. "I'm trying something in my classroom that really seems to be helping the kids. You've got to try it," she exclaimed. That "something" was her idea for using mentor texts in reference books to help kids follow up and be held accountable for strategies taught. In the beginning of this writing journey, Kristin would model a strategy in either a whole group or a small group, using a mentor text as an example. She would assume, then, that the kids had it and move on from there. What she was noticing, though, was that even with a great text example, even with her great concise teaching, the kids still didn't seem to be following through with using the strategy as much as she had hoped. She realized they needed a more permanent reminder to keep them accountable. That was the day her reference books were born. She simply took the mentor text that she had used as an example, shrank it down on a copier, and glued it into a construction-paper book. The reference books were titled *Elaboration* or *Voice* and each page contained a strategy for achieving that goal and the shrunk-down piece of text that showed what that strategy looked like in an actual piece of writing. Students also included examples of the strategy being used in their own writing pieces. Of course, like any good teacher does, Jen totally stole the idea and ran with it in her first-grade classroom. Instead of reference books, because Jen's first graders were not held accountable for as many strategies as Kristin's third graders, she created reference cards, using mentor text, with one strategy per card.

Where do we get the mentor text we use for the books and cards? We get the examples from the books in our classrooms, from library books, and from student writing that exemplifies the strategy. When we know what we want to teach, we search high and low for a great example that will not only model what we are asking the students to do but will keep the strategy vital and alive for our writers. We try to use as many student examples as possible to showcase the talent right in front of us. If students know that Sammy, for instance, has the strategy of using WOW words to elaborate, they can look at his example but also know he is a good person to go to when trying to revise for better word choice. Once the whole group, or even a small group of kids, uses the piece of text, we post the passage on a sticky note and then photocopy the text later in the day and use it to create the card or book. Sometimes the students help; other times we put it together quickly to save time and then show it to the class to remind them it is available.

How are these reference cards used and organized in the classroom? We keep the reference books/cards underneath the writing goals and strategies taught that hang on the classroom wall (or in Kristin's case, the window). Beneath each goal is a bin that holds the books or cards. We color-code the bins and cards to match the writing goal the cards go with. For example, the goal of elaboration is glued onto orange card stock, so the goals, reference cards, and the bin that holds them are all orange to match. This helps kids identify the strategies that will help them with the bigger goal. These reference tools are a great resource for whole- and small-group work to remind students of a strategy already taught. We put the reference books in this chapter because we also use them as a tool for making sure writers are actually using the strategy taught. We can quickly walk by a student who is working on using strong leads and drop the book or card next to him or her as a reminder and an example of what should be worked on. The best part is that even if we can't meet with the student that day, the follow-up is insinuated as soon as we put the card down next to the child. The message is, you've learned this, now please use it, here is how—we don't even have to say a word (Figure 5.12). The reference books and cards are also a great tool for helping us meet with kids. If

FIGURE 5.12
Taylor Uses the Reference Book to Help Her with the Conventional Rules of Dialogue.

a child is struggling with a strategy, the reference books and cards are there as a helping tool so we aren't interrupted as we work with other students.

It would be easy (and a lot less work) to create these reference books and then use them from year to year because "they are done." But to be effective, the books need to be created with the writers sitting in front of you, with their writing used as examples. You need to use mentor text passages that are familiar to them and chosen by them as great examples. There needs to be a strong connection for your writers to these books for them to truly be effective. Otherwise they just become another thing lying around your classroom. The books need to be dynamic, ever changing, and, as Kristin likes to say, dog-eared and covered with sticky fingerprints, to be the powerful tool we have found they can be for our young writers.

The idea of using mentor texts with writers is certainly not new. Since at least 2004, the National Council of Teachers of English (NCTE) has had a version of the following statement in their position statement on the teaching of writing:

> Writing and reading are related. People who engage in considerable reading often find writing an easier task, though the primary way a writer improves is through writing. Still, it's self-evident that to write a particular kind of text, it helps if the writer has read that kind of text, if only because the writer then has a mental model of the genre. In order to take on a particular style of language, it also helps to have read that language, to have heard it in her mind, so that she can hear it again in order to compose it. (NCTE 2016)

Up until this point, we had used a text as a model or active engagement tool but never really referenced it after the lesson was over. Once we began using reference books and cards, we saw how powerful they can be. One day during a writing assessment, Kristin was quick enough to grab her video camera and tape Logan, one of her most struggling writers, as he got up and walked over to the reference books (Figure 5.13). She taped him looking at the bins, picking up and setting down different books, until he found the one on leads he was looking for. He turned to the strategy he needed to start his piece, read the text example, and then went back to his seat to keep on writing.

FIGURE 5.13
Logan Grabs a Reference Book Before Heading Off to Write.

Jen brought her reference cards to a workshop she did at a conference in Las Vegas. After the session was finished, the teachers swarmed the cards to take pictures so they could take the idea back to their classrooms. This simple idea of not only using mentor text, but using it in a way that lasts and provides accountability to students, has been one of the best parts of our writing program. Both teachers and students become more accountable for using the writing strategies that support a broader goal. As Georgia Heard reminds us in her book *Finding the Heart of Nonfiction*, "In a writing community, a mentor text is literature that is used by writers to study craft and genre, and to inspire writing as well as vision" (2013, 3). We invite you to have the same experience within your writing community.

AUTHOR SHARE

Another way that we follow up with our writers to keep them accountable is through a daily author share. After we complete our writing time we ask one or two kids to share their writing with the class.

In Jen's room, the kids share their work aloud to receive their "glow" and "grow." After the child shares the piece, they all clap for the accomplishment of getting pen to paper and for simply being brave enough to put it all out there. Then Jen has the child hold up a page of the writing so everyone can admire it. The child calls on two children in the class. One child gives a "glow" or a compliment on what the writer is doing well. The second child offers up a "grow." This is either a suggestion of a way to improve the writing or a question to clarify something in the writing that was confusing. The author makes the final decision on whether he wants to revise his writing based on the suggestion or question, but even if the decision is made to leave the writing as it is, the idea is out there and there is a possibility he will try it in the next writing piece. The beginning of the school year is spent with the teacher's modeling "glows" and "grows" before the students begin to do it for each other. Just as we described in our discussion of partner work (Chapter 3), it is important that kids are explicitly taught how to give compliments and especially feedback in ways that are helpful, not hurtful. And as we suggested in the beginning of this book, before we have *students* offer suggestions for growth we spend a lot of time building trust in our classroom community. Once trust is established, the students begin to understand how the feedback is only to help them grow and not to diminish the work they have done as writers.

To follow up with the student and the writing goals that we have set together, Jen might ask a child who has reached a goal to share his work and then tell the class, "Niko has been working on adding dialogue to his writing. Let's listen to see if we hear the dialogue." Or she might say, "Niko, you have been working on adding dialogue into your writing as a way to elaborate. How is that going for you?" This way she is pushing Niko to be accountable for the goal he is trying to reach while reminding the rest of the writers in the class of a strategy they could be using as well in their own writing. Share time is a great opportunity to hold all the writers accountable for strategies taught. Usually the child sharing will bring a pen or pencil because as soon as the piece is read aloud, the revision begins. The child sharing will notice missing words, run-on sentences, or missing punctuation and will quickly fix it while sharing. It is quick and easy and a great reminder for the rest of the kids in the class of how important it is to read aloud their own writing and revise.

We can share in many different ways. We have learned that it is important to change the way we share to keep all of our students engaged. Sometimes Kristin has every writer choose one sentence that he or she is proud of and each writer gets to share. On other days Kristin and a small group share a new reference book they have created. Taylor and Matthew had been working on paragraphs. They each had a different challenge: Matthew had written only one paragraph for each chapter of his nonfiction book and Taylor had clear chapters but they were not in a logical order. Kristin had taught the class that in information writing they would need to create a new paragraph for each new idea or topic. After conferring with Matthew and Taylor, Kristin worked with them to make copies of their writing and build in pages to the paragraph book. Matthew showed the class what his writing looked like before he had paragraphs and what it looked like after he separated his writing into two chunks: what narwhals eat, and what eats narwhals. Taylor then shared her writing and explained to the class how she reorganized her paragraphs to keep like-minded topics together. Feeling empowered by new learning, Matthew and Taylor told the class that they would be happy to talk to other writers who were working on paragraphing.

Kristin also holds "silent sticky shares" at the end of writing time where writers leave a piece of writing on their desk and a classmate gets to read the writing and leave a sticky note with a compliment. Kristin challenges the writers to use specific compliments such as, "Your writing was so full of voice that I laughed out loud!" or "You did such a great job elaborating that I could picture everything you wrote about." She holds these shares randomly when she senses that her writers need an audience to give them purpose, to keep them engaged, or to celebrate at the end of a unit. Another version of the silent sticky share is to post student writing in the hallway and invite faculty or other classes to leave a written sticky note. This takes a little more preparation but it invites the outside world into the work.

Depending on the day and the time you have, there are many different ways you can have your students share their writing. Just make sure you build it in every day. Share time keeps the kids accountable for getting actual writing completed each day but also reminds them that they have an audience, and in the end that is what holds all of us as writers accountable. It is not only a way to celebrate but also a great way to follow up to make sure students are growing as writers and using the strategies that have been taught.

CELEBRATIONS

In our own lives we often treat ourselves when we have put a lot of time and effort into accomplishing a goal. We like to celebrate half marathons with mimosas, big life events often lead to a new Alex and Ani bracelet, and we can always justify a little shopping when we finish out the school year. When this book is completed, we are heading to Tahiti to lie on the beach . . . we wish!

In *Celebrating Writers* (2013), Ayres and Overman taught us a lot about what celebrating a writer's accomplishments should be and the difference between celebrations and publishing. They tell us, "Publication is part of the writing process. Celebration is part of the life of a writer" (2013, 5). We often used the

FIGURE 5.14
Celebrating Writing

two terms interchangeably, but what we have learned is that we can follow up with writers and hold them accountable for writing strategies learned by celebrating these accomplishments in every phase of the writing process—not just at the end when a piece goes public (Figure 5.14). Celebration plays a huge role in how we follow up with our kids. "Celebration allows writers to revel in their personal writing processes. It provides time for reflection and growth" (Ayres and Overman 2013, 5). This is everything we hope to accomplish when we teach our writers strategies that can help them grow and then hold them accountable for trying the strategies.

Writers can celebrate their writing in many ways, but it is really important to make the time to appreciate all the hard work that goes into composing a piece of writing. We try to create different celebrations so that we keep them fresh and exciting for our students. The purpose for the writing and the audience often guide the direction we head in when we plan a celebration. When our writers are writing to teach we want to give them an audience that they can teach. When writers are writing to persuade we want to provide the appropriate audience to persuade. Here are some of the ways that we celebrate with published pieces:

Who

- Sharing writing with parents
- Sharing writing with peers
- Sharing writing with younger students
- Sharing writing with older students
- Sharing with school principal, vice principal, P.E. teachers, or next year's teachers
- Inviting an important person in a student's life to share writing with
- Posting writing online with a class Twitter account or a class Facebook account
- Sharing with published writers, government officials, or local businesses (This is great for persuasive units or anytime the writer is writing to implement change.)

What

- Writers read their writing out loud to a partner.
- Guests read writing that is displayed and leave a sticky note compliment.
- Guests take a museum walk around student writing and offer compliments.
- Students share with guests a class video where each writer shares a portion of his or her writing.
- If several grades are working on the same genre, guests can visit a schoolwide museum.

Where

- In the school library surrounded by the work of published writers
- At the local library or a bookstore surrounded by the work of published writers
- Meeting other writers for a school picnic
- Having another class come and buddy-up to share writing
- Having parents come to class
- Outside

Here are some of the ways we celebrate throughout the writing process:

- Use a student's writing as a mentor text for other students and in the reference books
- Leave encouraging sticky notes telling the writer places where the writing is working
- Have the class stop and listen to a writer share writing that works because of a strategy used
- Allow partners to share with each other

We want to make sure that our celebrations stay grounded in the actual writing that the students have created. We try to avoid too many bells and whistles that will distract from the work of the writer. Ayres and Overman remind all of us, "After all, this is the point of writing instruction in elementary school. Students are developing their skills as writers. We don't expect perfection. We expect growth.

It is critical for the learning and growth to be honored and celebrated—not only during publication but throughout the entire process—so students have the stamina to continue writing day in and day out" (2013, 6). When celebrating becomes all about a perfect piece of writing at the end of a unit, we begin to focus too much on the writing and not enough on the growing writer in front of us. We expect that kids will grow when they are taught new strategies in a focused and consistent way while being held accountable by celebrating the successful writing that comes with the application of the strategy.

We use many different ways to follow up with our writers to make sure we are making a difference—assessment, pulling small instructional groups, utilizing reference books, author shares, and celebrations. We hope these ideas and suggestions will spur you on to follow up with your writers as well. Our goal, as teachers, is to teach writing strategies consistently and clearly so they go from being strategies to natural routines. That is how we know writers own them. We believe these teaching practices will make a difference for you and your students as well.

Afterword

In the end we know that there are lots of ways to go about teaching writing in your classroom. We have shared what works for us in the hopes that it might work for you. Use all our ideas, or just steal a few. That's what this project was all about. NCTE reminds us that "writers do not accumulate process skills and strategies once and for all. They develop and refine writing skills throughout their writing lives" (NCTE 2016). So be humble, and try to remember that you are one year of the child's writing life. It is not *all* on you. Your job is to provide developmentally appropriate feedback and help that child become a better writer than when he came in to your class. We believe this book will give you a place to start and newfound confidence for talking about writing with kids.

As we said in the beginning of this book, one of our three core beliefs is that we have a responsibility as educators to be constantly growing both professionally and personally. This book is not finished, although it has gone to publication. Our thinking will change and grow with each new writing conference we have. We hope you will read this book and think, "I like this idea, but I will do it a little differently for my kids" or "If I could talk to Jen and Kristin, I would tell them about things that work for me that they didn't mention," or maybe, "I wish I could get more clarification on what they said about . . ."

Just as we want to be constantly growing, we want that for you as well. Teaching can be a lonely profession; professional talk with other adults gets boiled down to five-minute hallway conversations. But that's how we got started. Let's create a community of educators together. Join us on the website we created, www.literacychats.wordpress.com, or follow us on Twitter @jenmcdonough and @kristinack1 #youngwriters, and let's keep this conversation going. Let's share our struggles, our questions, and our own writing and become a community of teachers who want more for our kids. This book is merely a starting point to the work we can do together. So instead of saying, "The End," as most books do, we extend an invitation for further growth and say simply, "Let's talk again!" See you soon!

REFERENCES

Anderson, Jeff. 2011. *10 Things Every Writer Needs to Know*. Portland, ME: Stenhouse.

Ayres, Ruth, and Christi Overman. 2013. *Celebrating Writers: From Possibilities Through Publication*. Portland, ME: Stenhouse.

Ayres, Ruth, and Stacey Shubitz. 2010. *Day by Day: Refining Writing Workshop Through 180 Days of Reflective Practice*. Portland, ME: Stenhouse.

Black, Michael Ian. 2010. *A Pig Parade Is a Terrible Idea*. New York: Simon and Schuster.

Bomer, Katherine. 2010. *Hidden Gems: Naming and Teaching from the Brilliance in Every Student's Writing*. Portsmouth, NH: Heinemann.

Boushey, Gail, and Joan Moser. 2009. *The CAFE Book: Engaging All Students in Daily Literacy Assessment and Instruction*. Portland, ME: Stenhouse.

———. 2014. *The Daily 5: Fostering Literacy Independence in the Elementary Grades*. 2d ed. Portland, ME: Stenhouse.

Brinckloe, Julie. 1985. *Fireflies*. New York: Aladdin Paperbacks.

Cali, Kathleen. 2013. *The Five Features of Effective Writing*. Available online at http://www.learnnc.org/lp/editions/few/680.

Calkins, Lucy. 1994. *The Art of Teaching Writing*. New ed. Portsmouth, NH: Heinemann.

———. 2013. *Writing Pathways: Performance Assessments and Learning Progressions*. Portsmouth, NH: Heinemann.

Calkins, Lucy, Amanda Hartman, and Zoe White. 2005. *One to One: The Art of Conferring with Young Writers*. Portsmouth, NH: Heinemann.

Corgill, Ann Marie. 2008. *Of Primary Importance: What's Essential in Teaching Young Writers*. Portland, ME: Stenhouse.

Cruz, M. Colleen. 2004. *Independent Writing: One Teacher—Thirty-Two Needs, Topics, and Plans*. Portsmouth, NH: Heinemann.

Culham, Ruth. 2005. *6 + 1 Traits of Writing: The Complete Guide for the Primary Grades.* New York: Scholastic.

Donohue, Lisa. 2011. *The Write Voice: Using Rich Prompts to Help Student Writing Come Alive.* Markham, ON: Pembroke.

Fletcher, Ralph, and JoAnn Portalupi. 2001. *Writing Workshop: The Essential Guide.* Portsmouth, NH: Heinemann.

Gallagher, Hugh. 1990. "3A Essay." Scholastic Art and Writing Awards. blog.artandwriting.org/wp-content/uploads/2012/08/Gallagher—3A-Essay.pdf.

Gallagher, Kelly. 2011. *Write Like This: Teaching Real-World Writing Through Modeling and Mentor Texts.* Portland, ME: Stenhouse.

Glover, Matt. 2009. *Engaging Young Writers: Preschool–Grade 1.* Portsmouth, NH: Heinemann.

Graves, Donald, and Penny Kittle. 2005. *Inside Writing: How to Teach the Details of Craft.* Portsmouth, NH: Heinemann.

Heard, Georgia. 1999. *Awakening the Heart: Exploring Poetry in Elementary and Middle School.* Portsmouth, NH: Heinemann.

———. 2013. *Finding the Heart of Nonfiction: Teaching 7 Essential Craft Tools with Mentor Texts.* Portsmouth, NH: Heinemann.

———. 2014. *The Revision Toolbox: Teaching Techniques That Work.* 2nd ed. Portsmouth, NH: Heinemann.

Jacobson, Jennifer. 2010. *No More "I'm Done!" Fostering Independent Writers in the Primary Grades.* Portland, ME: Stenhouse.

Landrigan, Clare, and Tammy Mulligan. 2013. *Assessment in Perspective: Focusing on the Reader Behind the Numbers.* Portland, ME: Stenhouse.

Lowry, Lois. 2009. *Crow Call.* New York: Scholastic.

McCranie, Stephen. 2011. *Mal and Chad: The Biggest, Bestest Time Ever!* New York: Philomel Books.

McDonough, Jennifer. 2012. "Enhance Reading Instruction with Student Reflections." In *Heinemann: Professional Development Services for K–12 Educators.* Fall Catalog-Journal.

Merriam-Webster. 2016. *Merriam-Webster Online.* S.v. "Structure." http://www.merriam-webster.com/dictionary/structure.

Miller, Donalyn. 2009. *The Book Whisperer: Awakening the Inner Reader in Every Child.* San Francisco: Jossey-Bass.

NCTE. 2016. "Professional Knowledge for the Teaching of Writing." Urbana, IL: National Council of Teachers of English. http://www.ncte.org/positions/statements/teaching-writing.

NGA/CCSSO (National Governors Association Center for Best Practices / Council of Chief State School Officers). 2010. *Common Core State Standards for English Language Arts and Literacy in History/Social Studies, Science, and Technical Subjects.* Washington, DC: NGA Center for Best Practices and CCSSO. http://www.corestandards.org/ELA-Literacy/.

Novak, B. J. 2014. *The Book with No Pictures.* New York: Penguin.

Overmeyer, Mark. 2005. *When Writing Workshop Isn't Working: Answers to Ten Tough Questions, Grades 2–5.* Portland, ME: Stenhouse.

———. 2015. *Let's Talk: One-on-One, Peer, and Small-Group Writing Conferences.* Portland, ME: Stenhouse.

Rader, Heather. 2016. "Finding a Fit." The Power of Conventions Series. https://www.choiceliteracy.com/articles-detail-view.php?id=1373.

Routman, Regie. 2005. *Writing Essentials: Raising Expectations and Results While Simplifying Teaching.* Portsmouth, NH: Heinemann.

INDEX